MARCO POLO

EDINBURGH

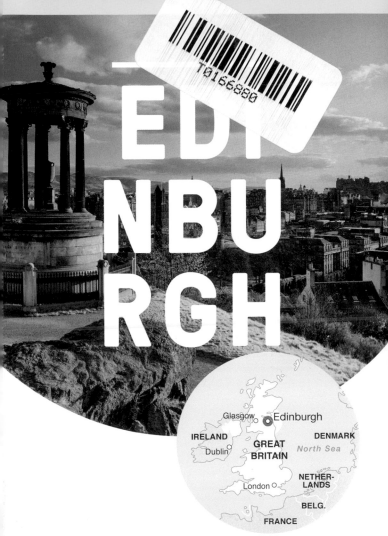

Glasgow • Edinburgh
IRELAND
Dublin
GREAT
BRITAIN
DENMARK
North Sea
London
NETHER-
LANDS
BELG.
FRANCE

THE TOURING APP

shows you the way ...
including routes and offline maps!

FREE!

GET MORE OUT OF YOUR MARCO POLO GUIDE

IT'S AS SIMPLE AS THIS

1 go.marcopolo.com/edi

2 download and discover

GO!

WORKS OFFLINE!

SYMBOLS

INSIDER TIP Insider Tip

★ Highlight

●●●● Best of...

☼ Scenic view

♲ Responsible travel: for eco-
logical or fair trade aspects

(*) Telephone numbers
that are not toll-free

PRICE CATEGORIES HOTELS

Expensive over £125

Moderate £80–125

Budget under £80

The prices are for a double
room per night, without
breakfast

PRICE CATEGORIES RESTAURANTS

Expensive over £35

Moderate £15–35

Budget under £15

The prices are for a three-
course meal without drinks

On the cover: View from Calton Hill p. 41 | The city at Festival time p. 96

CONTENTS

DID YOU KNOW?
Heart of Midlothian → p. 32
Time to chill → p. 38
Fit in the city → p. 42
For bookworms & film buffs → p. 48
Favourite eateries → p. 54
Local specialities → p. 56
More than a good night's sleep → p. 78
National holidays → p. 97
Spotlight on sports → p. 102
Weather → p. 104

MAPS IN THE GUIDEBOOK
(108 A1) Page numbers and coordinates refer to the street atlas
Coordinates are also given for places that are not marked on the street atlas
(0) Site/address located off the map
(🛆 A–B 2–3) refers to the removable pull-out map
General map Edinburgh and surroundings on p. 116/117

INSIDE FRONT COVER:
The best Highlights

INSIDE BACK COVER:
Public transport map

The best MARCO POLO Insider Tips

Our top 15 Insider Tips

INSIDER TIP **Let your Celtic hair down**
At the *Beltane Fire Festival* held on the last day of April, more than 12,000 people go on a pagan, Celtic spree that doesn't end until May. A really spectacular event on Calton Hill (photo right) → **p. 96**

INSIDER TIP **Bird's eye view**
Fantastic view over Royal Mile from the dizzying height of the roof of a safe haven: *St Giles Cathedral* → **p. 38**

INSIDER TIP **From bean to bar**
If you want to find out why chocolate is healthy, contact *The Chocolate Tree* well in advance to attend one of its events where you can learn everything about the production and enjoyment of chocolate → **p. 52**

INSIDER TIP **William Turner likes it gloomy**
The *National Gallery* only exhibits some of the artist's watercolours in the weak January light to prevent them from fading → **p. 46**

INSIDER TIP **Pandas and penguins**
Besides the daily penguin parade in *Edinburgh Zoo* (photo above), there's one more highlight: giant pandas → **p. 94**

INSIDER TIP **Cryptic crypt**
Non-stop horror films, pole dancing, cosy corners and "candlelight burgers" in the gloomy *Banshee Labyrinth* under a bridge in the Old Town → **p. 69**

INSIDER TIP **Seaweed brew**
You will be able to try a drink you have definitely never had before at the *David Bann* vegetarian restaurant: beer made of seaweed → **p. 55**

INSIDER TIP **A hat for every head**
Perhaps a Sherlock Holmes-style deerstalker for his lordship and surely nothing but a fascinator will do for her ladyship – a hatter and her universe rule in *Fabhatrix* in the heart of Old Town → **p. 62**

INSIDER TIP **Dessert with a steely soft drink**

Irn-Bru, the orange-coloured Scottish pick-me-up and national soft drink, is the basis of one of the desserts served in the *Hotel du Vin Bistro* → **p. 55**

INSIDER TIP **A gardener's love**

Without the Michelin cherry on top, yet classy and creative, *The Gardener's Cottage* serves five-course meals on long tables without veering into opulence → **p. 81**

INSIDER TIP **Celebrate in Scottish style**

The people of Edinburgh have storytelling and music in their blood. The Scottish-Gaelic culture is joyfully celebrated at Easter at the *TradFest* → **p. 96**

INSIDER TIP **Feel at home**

You can rent a holiday flat behind the thick walls on *Candlemaker Row* – in the midst of the hustle and bustle of the Old Town near Greyfriars' Cemetery with its tales of vanishing corpses → **p. 78**

INSIDER TIP **Forward looking**

The large clock on the tower next to Waverley Station is two minutes fast so that passengers won't miss their train – the only exception is on New Year's Eve → **p. 44**

INSIDER TIP **Breathtaking panorama**

You will get the best photo of the castle from *St Cuthbert's Cemetery* at the foot of the hill. It is particularly beautiful in winter when leaves do not block your view → **p. 45**

INSIDER TIP **Under your skin**

The arrival of fresh corpses – supplied by grave robbers and murderers – was once eagerly anticipated at *Surgeons' Hall*. Some would stop at literally nothing in the service of science. Today it's possible to explore the inside of the body without a scalpel – using the simple touch technology of the converted dissecting iTable → **p. 39**

BEST OF...

FOR FREE

● *Three-hour declaration of love to the city*
You will have certainly fallen in love with Edinburgh after this *free tour* of the metropolis. The enthusiastic guides are devoted to their city and know absolutely everything about haunted houses and spitting, inventions and striving for independence, about music making, etc, etc, etc. ... → p. 36

● *Secret Festival favourite*
Originally, the *Festival Fringe* was just an offshoot of the Edinburgh International Festival. But for some years now, visitors have not only been attracted to the many comedy and theatre performances just because they're free (photo) → p. 20

● *First the sheep and then the kilt*
Would you like to find out how a kilt is made? The *Tartan Weaving Mill & Exhibition* will provide you with all the answers → p. 36

● *Scotland in session*
The *Scottish Parliament* looks like an upturned ship but this visionary construction fits perfectly into the tightly-knit Old Town. You can satisfy your curiosity about the cryptic architecture on a free tour → p. 37

● *Edinburgh's famous writers*
Burns, Scott and Stevenson are shining stars in the Scottish literature firmament. The memorabilia in the small *Writers' Museum* will give you an idea of the time they spent in Edinburgh → p. 39

● *Modern art from Scotland's capital*
The *Scottish National Gallery of Modern Art Two* (next to Gallery One) pays homage to Edinburgh's greatest artist – Eduardo Paolozzi: sculptor, Surrealist, Pop-Artist → p. 48

● *Jazz for free*
The Jazz Bar swings more than any other club in town. From Tuesday to Sunday evening, free, un-plugged sessions until 7.30pm at the bar's "Teatime Acoustics" events → p. 72

◖◗◗◗ Dots in guidebook refer to "Best of..." tips

● *The castle on the volcano*

The most impressive aspect of *Edinburgh Castle* and the volcanic rock it is built on is the silhouette the two merge to form. The crown jewels and the Stone of Destiny in the castle are true gems. The views are breathtaking! → p. 30

● *Memento mori*

The gloomy *Greyfriars Cemetery* in the heart of the Old Town is like a history book of the city carved in stone. A lot of people come here because they believe the place is haunted. The corpse thieves Burke and Hare dug up bodies buried here for an anatomy professor → p. 32

● *Fiddles in the bar*

Sandy Bell's is a pub with a resounding reputation. There is nothing more typically Scottish than listening to folk musicians at a jam session with a glass of beer in your hand → p. 72

● *Eating in the heart of the city*

You will feel like you are in a catacomb in the vaults of *The Grain Store* restaurant. Tuck into the unpretentious food served by candlelight in what was once a warehouse → p. 57

● *Just a department store?*

Jenners, from 1838, does not try to be modern. Here a small escalator, there a narrow, winding staircase. You can never be quite sure which of the 100 departments on the six floors you will find yourself in – but Jenners sells absolutely everything (photo) → p. 61

● *Farmer's market with a view of the castle*

The best market in the country is quite simply named *Farmer's Market*. Sixty farmers and producers offer their exquisite, out of the ordinary produce for sale on Saturday: wild boar, organic beer, ostrich and water-buffalo meat, lobster, honey, chutneys ... → p. 64

● *Royal-tea!*

You too can extend your little finger while sipping at a cup of tea in these hallowed halls. According to King George IV, the famous *Signet Library* was the finest of Britain's assembly rooms. Time for high tea! → p. 51

ONLY IN

BEST OF...

● *Play of light in the Cathedral*
The play of light created by the glass windows and modern glass curtain behind the entrance to *St Giles Cathedral* will even fascinate you if the weather is typically Scottish. Watch out for the carved angel playing bagpipes → p. 38

● *The haunted lane underneath the pavement*
The Real Mary King's Close is the lane to end all lanes. This piece of the city's history is underground today and gives an authentic and gruesome impression of life in the Middle Ages → p. 35

● *Classicist temple of the arts*
The Classicist *Scottish National Gallery* shows world-famous works alongside Scottish highlights. It is worth visiting the Gallery just to see Henry Raeburn's fabulous painting "The Skating Minister" → p. 45

● *What a ship!*
Rule Britannia, Britannia rule the waves – the royal yacht, with its Art Deco interior, is no longer in service and is now anchored at Leith. A sensual feast for the eyes with the flair of the seas (photo) → p. 48

● *At the preacher's house*
John Knox was the rhetorical spearhead of the Scottish Reformation and Mary Stuart's opponent. Listen to the debates between the preacher and the Catholic Queen of Scots. The fantastic Scottish Storytelling Centre is also based here → p. 33

● *Take the train to the Aquarium*
Not only children will love the *Deep Sea World* underwater zoo – especially if you travel there by train from Waverley Station across the famous Firth of Forth Bridge → p. 94

RAIN

RELAX AND CHILL OUT
Take it easy and spoil yourself

● *Seduced by a chocolate Buddha*
Sumptuous, sinful, seductive – you should take some time out at *The Chocolate Tree* boutique to try the ginger Buddhas coated in cocoa or Venetian masks that melt in your mouth → **p. 52**

● *An evening view from the volcano*
You will have the most beautiful view if you look down on the city from the Greek columns on *Calton Hill* at twilight. Don't forget the sundowner → **p. 41**

● *Classical music in the church*
The *Greyfriars Kirk* has been through a lot; it was even a gunpowder warehouse in the 18th century and immediately blew up! It is now considerably more peaceful in the beautifully restored interior. The regular concerts of classical music are particularly atmospheric → **p. 33**

● *Cinematic beauty*
The old décor of the *Cameo Picturehouse* is a picture itself; take a seat in auditorium 1 with a drink from the bar and ample legroom to enjoy an arthouse movie or silent film → **p. 71**

● *Elegant living*
You will really be able to relax in one of the spacious flats behind the historical façade of the *Chester Residence*. There is round-the-clock service to take care of your every wish → **p. 75**

● *The pool above town*
Go up to the roof of the Sheraton Grand: At the *One Spa,* you will be able to unwind in an outdoor pool with a panoramic view of the city → **p. 38**

● *Oasis of green in the city*
The *Princes Street Gardens* on the south side of the Old Town are Edinburgh's solarium. In summer this oasis of la dolce vita is treated to music from the Ross Bandstand; towards the end of the year it's Christmas market time (photo) → **p. 43**

CHILL OUT

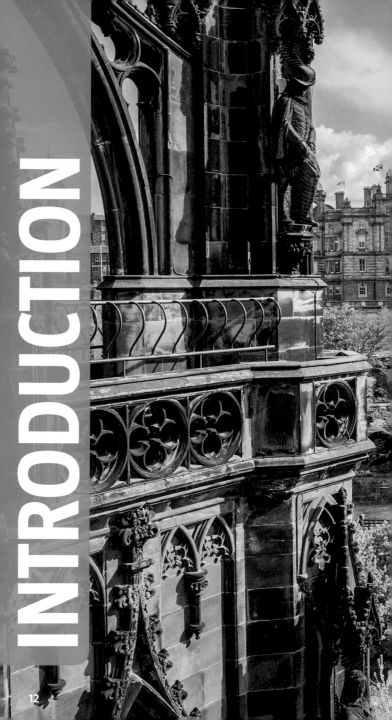

INTRODUCTION

DISCOVER
EDINBURGH!

As a small capital city on the edge of Europe, Edinburgh cannot play first fiddle in the global city orchestra – at the most, it could play the loudest bagpipe. For a long time, many visitors merely considered the city as the gateway to the Highlands. But with the establishment of a regional parliament, this sleeping beauty started to awaken from its years of slumber. Its numerous festivals have now been joined by new restaurants with Michelin stars, fashion houses and boutiques, the revamping of the port and one of the most sensational parliament buildings in Europe. Direct flights from many European airports have made Edinburgh a perfect destination for an urban holiday.

This city is a real *natural talent*. Volcanism and ice ages left behind a rugged hilly land-scape on the estuary of the Firth of Forth, into which the compact metropolis is organically embedded. A royal castle from the 7th century, perched like an eyrie on a hill, marked its beginnings, and the city started to develop around Edinburgh Castle – which rises high into the sky above the city. Seen from one of the three hills in the city, the dramatic *skyline of the Old Town* at sunset creates one of the most atmospheric portraits of any European metropolis. Active city strollers treat themselves to a picnic on Calton Hill – after having climbed up all the way.

Edinburgh – and Scotland – have one man in particular to thank that this remote beauty on the edge of the Highlands did not remain a place known only to insiders over the past 200 years. In the 19th century, the author *Walter Scott* took a story of a not terribly imposing man-at-arms and wove legends, bloody battles between the English and the Scots, and tragic love stories from the Highlands into a web of historical novels. The prose that flowed from Scott's pen is possibly not the most refined, but readers throughout Europe couldn't get enough of it. And thus they started travelling to Scotland. Writers from the Continent felt that Edinburgh's geography and *Neoclassicist architecture* invested it with the aura of an "Athens of the North". Scottish tourism and Hollywood's *Highlander* films would be inconceivable without Scott. The same applies to the cult of the kilt. Scott turned the skirt-like piece of clothing worn by the Highlanders – that had become scorned after an inglorious defeat by the English – into a fashionable garment when he invited King George IV to Edinburgh in 1822 and put him in a kilt, too.

Bloody battles, wild legends and the cult of the kilt

Edinburgh's plus points are not limited to its magnificent location and tartans. The authoritarian church reformer John "Killjoy" Knox brought *Calvinism* to Catholic-oriented Edinburgh in 1560 and subjected the nation to his "Book of Discipline". Edinburgh became the epicentre of a Scottish moral earthquake that made the church more independent from the Crown – in contrast to England, where the Reformation was less of a grass-roots affair. Edinburgh's Protestantism created institutions such as autonomous churches, law courts and schools.

Scotland's fate was ultimately decided at the beginning of the 18th century. In those days, Edinburgh felt it had similar colonisation powers to London and attempted to create a settlement in what is today Panama. *New Caledonia* ended in financial disaster however, making Scotland bankrupt. Partly due to a lack of English support and partly from the Scots falling into London's arms: The *Act of Union* from 1707 united both countries under the leadership of London. The merger, however, helped Scotland be a part of the *expansion of the United Kingdom* and promote the country's talents.

The emerging Scottish Age of Enlightenment resulted in the first faculty of medicine in Great Britain being established in Edinburgh in 1726, followed by a philosophical society in 1739. Adam Smith, the father of economic theory, was from Edinburgh – in Voltaire's opinion, the city was one of Europe's main intellectual centres for a time.

At the same time, Edinburgh, with around 50,000 inhabitants living in cramped conditions in ten-to-twelve storey buildings, stank to high heaven – the well-to-do citizens downstairs, the poorer souls above. The sum of the day's calls of nature was unceremoniously poured out of the window into the alley below at bedtime. If you threw your tankard at the wall of a pub, or so it is said, it would stick to the filth on it. In spite of this, new ideas formed in these pubs. If you climb Calton Hill for a romantic *evening picnic*, you will find Edinburgh's skyline to your left hardly changed: In the background, the old castle with the densely populated medieval *Old Town* sweeping down from the hill top to the Palace of Holyroodhouse. On the right, a completely different city comes into view – also quite old by now. The Georgian *New Town*, built in around 1800, represents

The city with two faces – Dr. Jekyll and Mr Hyde

the *non plus ultra* of city planning of the period: uniform, precise, and spacious. The other half of Edinburgh was created in response to the overcrowding south of Nor Loch, a heavily polluted body of water in which witches had once been drowned. This

Duo in red: lonely letterbox against the railway bridge across the Firth of Forth

POST

3.45pm

drained lake is today the green heartland of Edinburgh: Princes Street Gardens separate the Old from the New Town and the medieval from the mundane. Nothing has really changed in Edinburgh since Walter Scott invited King George IV to New Town; an architectural triumph which has lasted for centuries.

With a population of approximately 500,000, Edinburgh is Scotland's second-largest city today. While the largest, Glasgow – only 50 minutes away by train – appears post-industrial, modernist and shirt-sleeved, the civil servants in the capital seem to prefer suits and ties. The millennium politics of the London Scot Tony Blair made it possible for Scotland to break away from its political union with England. Four fifths of all Scots voted in favour of *devolution* in 1997. The newly elected Scottish Parliament moved into its new residence in 2004. Designed by Catalan architect Enric Miralles, the modern Parliament Building is situated next to the Palace of Holyroodhouse and blends perfectly into its Old Town surroundings.

> **The new political agenda was aimed at independence from London**

And now? The union with England seems in greater danger than ever before. EU-friendly Scotland has juxtaposed itself politically with London – where policies are still elitist and neoliberal – in terms of social issues, education and the environment. Two thirds of Scots voted to remain in Europe in the 2016 Brexit referendum. After losing the closely run *independence referendum* in 2014, First Minister Nicola Sturgeon, currently the leader in Edinburgh, is waiting for the right time to try again – a vote that could ultimately spell the end for Great Britain after a union of over 300 years.

Glasgow has fought its way out if its industrial decline but Edinburgh still appears to be working on plans to develop a more contemporary profile in the coming years. City planners have to steer a course between change and the demands of a World Heritage Site, seeing that both the New and Old Town bear this coveted Unesco title. It comes as no surprise that the Scottish capital with its two hearts is always on the brink of a cardiac arrest during the *cultural festival month* of August. The population doubles and the iconic metropolis almost suffocates in this passionate embrace. The *creative urge* to foster the human spirit, which has not let the people of Edinburgh come to rest since the Enlightenment, erupts with full force in the Edinburgh International Festival and the Festival Fringe – the biggest cultural gatherings in the world, but for party-loving Edinburgh only the climax of a year riddled with festivals.

It is fairly easy to explore the Scottish capital on foot – if you don't get lost. You will find yourself continuously going up and down hills and steps, and over rough cobblestones. Take sturdy shoes with you. Strolling around the carefully laid-out streets in the New Town is an easy affair but the Old Town is almost reminiscent of one of the impossible staircase constructions in drawings by the Dutch artist M. C. Escher.

Climb up or take a break? Summer-time questions at the Scott Monument

Don't hesitate to ask locals the way – this could lead to a shortcut through a romantic cemetery. In conversation with the residents of Edinburgh, you will be able to listen to the delights of the *Scottish accent* with its almost uncontrollable rolled vowels – an accent that has stumped many a foreigner. It has a lovely ring to it and is nowhere nearly as difficult as Glaswegian. However, if you arrive in a

The magic of Edinburgh never fades

pub while there is a music session in full swing, it might be that you will not understand anything at all. In that case, you will have hit on Gaelic singing. And what a stroke of luck. You will have come across the true Scottish soul of Edinburgh somewhere in the catacombs of the capital.

This metropolis, which is both grotesquely Gothic and classically hip, has an enchanting air about it unlike virtually any other. And just when you start thinking about leaving this magic behind you, you will hear the sound of bagpipes echoing down the streets. So don't even try to entertain such thoughts: you can pack your bags whenever you want, check out of your hotel and set off for home – but Edinburgh will never really let you out of its spell!

WHAT'S HOT

1 A feast for the eyes

Café and art Gastronomy and arts form a perfect symbiosis in the *City Art Centre Café (2 Market Street)*. Everything is first rate and will make you want more. Not only artists who have their studios there get together in the *Drill Hall Arts Café (36 Dalmeny Street | www.outoftheblue.org.uk/cafe)*. You can really feel the creativity in the air. And, not only the kitchen is creative at *Henderson's (25c Thistle Street | www.hendersonsofedinburgh.co.uk)*; the oldest vegetarian restaurant in Great Britian also has its own gallery.

DRILL HALL

Drink in the atmosphere at Edinburgh's new arts café in The **Out of the Blue** Drill Hall. Relax with a fair trade ... of wine or cup of coffee ... taking in an exhibition ... rmance. Enjoy freshly ... local produce und ... stic sweep of t ... and steel-span ... t with over ... at this ... onve ... tre ...

Adventurous 2

Sport with an adrenalin boost Abseiling 165 feet off the *Forth Rail Bridge (www.ultimate abseil.com) (photo)* in June and October is not only a huge kick, but also supports the charity Chest Heart & Stroke Scotland. Also very popular: in *Survival of the Fittest (ratrace.com/survival/teams)*, participants form teams and race each other, for example along the Royal Mile. Ratho *Edinburgh International Climbing Arena (short.travel/edi27)* is Europe's biggest indoor climbing venue, with climbing, bouldering and much more.

3 Slippery fun

Bowls on ice What brings together yoga stretching, high-intensity scrubbing, blade-less ice skating and board game tactics in a fun team sport? Curling! The sport was invented in Scotland 500 years ago and is currently enjoying a comeback. Edinburghers amuse themselves from September to March with indoor curling at *Murrayfield Curling Rink (edinburghcurlingschool.org.uk | 2 hour taster course £10) (photo)*.

Green sports

A workout for do-gooders Is a visit to the zoo still ethically tenable? *Edinburgh Zoo* offers you a chance to give something back when you spend three or six hours feeding, mucking out and caring for the animals with a professional keeper *(from £150 | short.travel/edi 24)*. Is cycling a green sport? Of course; but the *Pedals* bike shop *(39 Barclay Place | www.pedals-edinburgh.com)* makes it even more environmentally friendly. 🌐 The shop, which is furnished with recycled furniture, repairs bikes rather than disposing of them and uses biodegradable lubricants and as many used spare parts as possible to achieve this.

4

Tried and true

Vintage fashion They are more than just a passing fad: the small, exquisite second-hand shops in the city centre are a way of life. Not only do clients rediscover trends that have survived the passing of time, they also invest in a good cause when they shop at *Barnardo's Vintage (106 Nicolson Street | www.barnardos. org.uk)*, which used to be known as the Salvation Army. *Godiva (9 West Port | www. godivaboutique.co.uk) (photo)* not only has cool second-hand things to wear but also clothing from the *Edinburgh College of Art* – in this way, you can support up-and-coming designers. You will find unconventional, flashy and beautiful clothing at *Herman Brown (151 West Port | www.her manbrown.co.uk)* that specialises in fashion and accessories from the last decades: dresses from the Forties up until today, bags, jewellery, gloves and scarves. A paradise for retro fans!

5

IN A NUTSHELL

A CITY CELEBRATES

Edinburghers are party animals — and there has been reason enough to party every month in Edinburgh since Viennese emigrant Sir Rudolf Bing initiated the now world-famous ★ *Edinburgh International Festival (EIF)* as a platform for intellectual blossoming in 1947. All genres of music, the sciences, pagan-Celtic customs and even the art of storytelling are all fitting focuses for festivals. In the merry month of August, the population of the global party capital doubles, when half a dozen festivals take place simultaneously. Quirky theatre enchants living rooms, while serious plays fill the larger stages. At the same time, legions of street artists juggle and tumble through the alleyways, like thou-sands of cultural ruffians drilling a rebellion against small-mindedness, war and smart-arsedness. *Delirium edinburghiensis* is extremely infectious. Today the EIF is recognised as the largest cultural festival in the world as it attracts around 2 million visitors to the city. Yet it is only one of many events held in August. The ★ ● *Edinburgh Festival Fringe (www.edfringe.com, www.freefestival.co.uk)* is an offshoot to the EIF and is a real crowd-puller not just because many of the events offer free admission.

A ULD ALLIANCE

Embassies are still not allowed in Edinburgh, but the French already set up a consulate in the Old Town and hoisted the tricolour in 2017. A curious

Where top spies deliver milk, men wear skirts and queens end up in prison – *Edinbarra* is all that and much more

amour fou, this Franco-Scottish alliance, strengthened through skirmishes with England, initiated by Mary Stuart's formative years in France? At least the affair was long lasting, regally guaranteed for 300 years and well-founded in a common hatred of England. But when Edinburgh threw itself into London's arms at the start of the 18th century, became Protestant and cast its lot in with Great Britain, the Auld Alliance was passé. Edinburgh recovered, pulled itself kicking and screaming out of the swamp of the medieval Old Town and up into the blossoming enlightenment of the New Town. Even Voltaire noticed this – he saw Edinburgh at the time as a civilising role model! Today you will see many Scottish cars adorned with "Écosse" signs – French for Scotland. It must be love!

BAGPIPES

There are strong differences of opinion about the sounds that come out of these squawking, bellicose bags that are still played in many armies. But fact and myth clash as well – something typically Scottish. After the final battle for Scotland in Culloden in 1745, pipers were sentenced to death because the court martial classified bagpipes as weapons. This led to the rumour that the English would impose the death penalty on anybody playing the pipes. That there were not enough pupils at piping schools had more to do with the fact that the clan chieftains had become too impoverished to pay for lessons. And that, even in modern day Edinburgh, cases come to court of people accused of disturbing the peace, is also true. In a bizarre case, a piper in London had to pay a fine for noisemaking. The court refused to accept that the death penalty, imposed on a piper in 1745, could be taken as a precedent and ruled that the bagpipe was indeed a musical instrument. The plaintiff, who saw his bagpipes more as a weapon, decided not to appeal when the judge informed him that the alternative would be to be charged with the illegal possession of arms! The traditional Highland bagpipes are played using a nine-note scale. The bag is made of leather or occasionally Gore-Tex. They were already used by the Romans and today there are still dozens of different varieties of these shepherds' pipes around the world. This powerful noisemaker (130 decibels!) has many different names – some, such as the Finnish *säkkipilli*, are just as weird as the sound the instrument produces.

C OOL SCOTLAND

The British press, never known to be short of a slogan, invented the term "Cool Britannia", based loosely on the closet national anthem "Rule, Britannia!", 20 years ago. The zeitgeist phrase was created to describe Tony Blair and the way he seemed to surround himself with stars of pop music and art. But the British premier was actually born in Edinburgh, and later attended its famous Fettes College. Reason enough to check for other phenomenal personalities that attest to Scotland's coolness. Sean Connery! He delivered milk to Fettes College. After being persuaded of Connery's coolness as the first James Bond, Ian Fleming went on to ascribe the fictional character an education at the selfsame college. Connery is fairly old, still cool and a supporter of the rebellious Scottish National Party which for this reason alone makes the party cool.

The list of cool Scots is endless: without John Boyd Dunlop, air-filled tyres and, as a consequence, cars would never have been invented. Without waterproof clothing from Charles Mackintosh, we would still be standing in the rain. Since the deaf Alexander Graham Bell invented the telephone, we can talk to everyone around the globe. Without Annie Lennox, we would never have known how cool women can be. Yet that Edinburgh harbours a darker, uncool side to its personality has been apparent since Ian Rankin sent out his Detective Inspector Rebus to solve crimes in and around the city and which Robert Louis Stevenson had uncovered with the brutal murders committed by his Dr Jekyll alias Mr Hyde. Irvine Welsh also depicted a pacy yet destructive portrayal of some Edinburgh individuals in his novel "Trainspotting".

C URRENCY

Strictly speaking, Scottish pound notes are not legal tender. In spite of this, the Scottish version of the British pound accounts for around 95 percent of payments in Scotland. In contrast to the way things are done south of the border, the three largest Scottish banks distribute the banknotes. The three sets have different designs showing bridges, castles and famous Scots. The most-printed portrait is that of Sir Walter

Tartan kilts in step at the famous Military Tattoo

Scott. It is often difficult to pay with these notes – in denominations between 5 and 100 pounds – outside Scotland. Scotland does not mint its own coins. With a bit of luck, you might get hold of one of the Scottish one-pound notes that have now become rare – so keep it as a souvenir!

SCOTLAND FOR THE SCOTS

At the moment, the Scots must feel like they're living in a Highlander film, while its direction is increasingly slipping out of their hands. First Tony Blair's devolution policy meant that Edinburgh once again had a mature parliament after centuries without. The left-leaning liberal Scottish National Party SNP soon surpassed the old guard and now governs the country from an epic and rather cool seat of parliament. But the attempt to separate from Great Britain (per independence referendum) narrowly failed in 2014. In the last chapter of the drama, for the time being, the Scots were forced to submit to the Brexit vote in 2016, even though they had voted against leaving the EU. Most feel disenfranchised once again – there is no way they want to break from the EU, partly because Scotland's economy depends on EU subsidies and EU migrants.

Quo vadis, Scotland? The resolute head of government, Nicola Sturgeon, is flirting with another referendum – which London would first have to authorise! – but was sent a clear message in the British general elections in 2017 that clever Scottish voters are hoping for a soft Brexit first. So Edinburgh is not turning up the heat on the British thriller for the time being. Instead London's political gambling has been treated to caustic sarcasm with the production of a Brexit musical for the Fringe that exposed the absurdity of the "leave" advocates. In the meantime the tug of war between heroines Nicola and Theresa (May) continues. All possible finales are still imaginable, except perhaps the beheading that ended the feud between Queen Elizabeth I and Mary, Queen of Scots back in the 16th century.

SCOTTISH

Scottish English sounds like a dialect but, from a linguistic point of view, it is quite different: Scottish is precisely the English spoken throughout Scotland as the national language of education. *Scots*, on the other hand, is much more of a dialect and is spoken by around one third of the Scots – especially in the southern parts of the country. It is not a literary language as there are no rules for its spelling. *Scots* is classified as a regional and minority language in Europe. Writers, such as the classic Robert Burns and the contemporary Irvine Welsh, write what is spoken as they hear it, phonetically. Scottish Gaelic – Celtic – is a completely different matter; it was brought to Scotland by Irish immigrants many centuries ago. No matter where you come from, you should not forget that Edinburgh is always pronounced with a Scottish rasp as "Edinbarra"!

TARTAN & KILT

The Gaelic word *tartan* means a checked cloak made of woollen fabric.

Used as an adjective, it can also allude to Scotland or the Scots as in the case of a *tartan tax*. The most famous piece of clothing that is made of it has its roots in the old-Scandinavian word *kilt*.

In the 17th century, the Scots discovered the checked tunic once worn by the Celts for themselves. Approximately 6 to 8 yards of single-width (26–30 inches), or 3 to 4 yards of double-width cloth (54–60 inches) are needed to make a modern kilt; the pattern is determined by the clan the wearer belongs to. The cool weather in Scotland makes wearing knee-high socks vital and a small knife, the Sgian Dubh, is traditionally tucked into the right one (or the left, if the wearer is left-handed). This was appropriate clothing for the poor inhabitants of the rough terrain of the Highlands that they were forced to give up after they had lost the Battle of Culloden. But, from 1815, the kilt made a reappearance and King George IV wore one when he visited Edinburgh in 1822. The patterns were registered and, since then, there has

State-of-the-art architecture: the debating chamber in the Scottish Parliament

been no stopping the triumphant progress of the checked woollen fabric. Organisations such as Amnesty International, the Royal Family and even the former Pope Benedict XVI, who visited Edinburgh in September 2010, have their own tartans. Men usually attend Scottish weddings in – sometimes borrowed – kilts. One question remains to be answered: what do they wear under the kilt? It can happen that the questioner is embarrassed when the wearer does a cartwheel to satisfy his or her curiosity.

THAT JEKYLL AND HYDE FEELING

Horror and glamour, day and night, beauty and the beast – these contrasts complement each other in the most sensual of ways in Edinburgh. On one side the medieval Old Town, hung spookily between two volcanic hills, on the other the finest of neo-classic chic – the architectural ensemble of New Town has been honoured with World Heritage status. Split personality disorder in the cityscape – nowhere else is as beautifully creepy as here.

Let's just call it the Jekyll and Hyde feeling, based loosely on the novel by the city's son Robert Louis Stevenson, in which a gentleman mutates into a rogue at nighttime. Scary walking tours and the 3-D effects of a *digital cadaver* convincingly conjure up a horrifying Edinburgh. It may also lead you underground, if you choose to descend into a high-quality reenactment at The Real Mary King's Close. Two days are recommended (at least), and in fact two different outfits, too. The narrow and steep consumptive alleys that riddle the Old Town are best tackled with cushioned soles under your feet. For the opulently planned 18th-century New Town, laboratory for Scotland's intellectual enlighten-

ment, pumps or leather shoes are the footwear of choice.

TWO QUEENS ARE ONE TOO MANY

She was a beauty, an enfant terrible with manners learnt at the French royal court where she was brought up, and she hid a pigskin football in her bedroom in Stirling – Mary Stuart, formerly Stewart. Edinburgh's most famous celebrity became Queen of Scots before she had even turned one year old. The fun-loving "It girl" with a foible for golf was, furthermore, Catholic, which drove her arch enemy and Edinburgh neighbour, the reformer John Knox, to preach angry sermons in St Giles Cathedral. You can listen to how the two of them argued over God and the world in reenacted dialogues in John Knox House. Politics personified, her protestant cousin Queen Elizabeth left Mary out in the cold for 19 years, before beheading her in 1587.

WHISKY

A document in the Edinburgh National Library proves it: in 1494, a certain John Cor ordered "8 bolls of malt to make aqua vitae". The noble single malt – a whisky made at a single distillery from a mash that uses one particular grain – was introduced about 400 years later but disappeared from the market before showing up again around 1960 as a drink for connoisseurs. Single Malt Whisky now accounts for approximately ten percent of all Scotch sold. Edinburgh is the malt capital and one of the best places to hunt for your favourite drop is on the Royal Mile. By the way, the Scottish "water of life" is called *uisge beatha*, which was subsequently shortened to *whisky*. Whatever you do, do not confuse this with the Irish or American varieties of *whiskey* written with an "e".

SIGHTSEEING

CITY | WHERE TO START?

It is easy to explore the Old and New Town on foot if you start at **Waverley Station (110 B6)** *(𝄞 F4)*. A flight of steps leads to the Royal Mile, where the Castle, the Parliament and the Palace of Holyroodhouse can be found. The elegant shops on George Street and St Andrew Square in the New Town are also only a five-minute walk from Waverley. Underground car park at Waverley Station, New Street. From the airport: a tram runs every ten minutes to Princes Street and the station (35 min, £5.50).

Edinburgh is like a stage set, not a modern metropolis. Climb up one of the three steep volcanic hills in the centre and you will see two completely different inner cities at your feet – from two periods – but hardly any modern architecture.

Seen from 🚲 Edinburgh Castle, the urban drama that unfolds below could be a thriller in a romantic setting that has inspired writers in their creativity for centuries. Go down into the splendid theatre, make your entrance on stage, and become a performer and member of the audience at the same time.

Once you reach the bottom, everything is within easy walking distance – and there is no need to rush. If you are in a hurry, you will miss what is the most amazing aspect of the individual districts – their astonish-

Streets that breathe history in the Old Town and urban elegance in the New Town – a contrasting picture of Edinburgh

ing architectural homogeneity. Edinburgh has many intimate corners where you will quite tangibly feel what is lying beneath the surface of the city. So don't overlook any well-trodden stepped streets, don't miss a single cemetery, and grasp every opportunity to have a chat with the locals. The urban compactness of the Old Town is only broken by the bridge that sweeps north to Edinburgh's main Waverley Station. The only breach in the phalanx of houses has been created in 2004 by the Scottish Parliament Building – a modern,

controversial architectural masterpiece – in the lower section of the Old Town.

However, Edinburgh can also appear quite arrogant at times; especially where the New Town seems to consciously show off its architectural uniqueness. You should walk through the gorgeous Princes Street Gardens on your way to the fascinating villa city from 1820. Robert Louis Stevenson grew up here in the Georgian New Town and he immortalised the hybrid nature of his hometown in his novel about the good-natured Dr. Jekyll who turned into

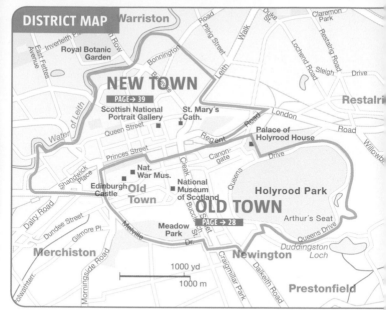

DISTRICT MAP

PAGE → 39

NEW TOWN

Royal Botanic Garden

Scottish National Portrait Gallery

St. Mary's Cath.

Palace of Holyrood House

Nat. War Mus.

Edinburgh Castle

Old Town

National Museum of Scotland

OLD TOWN

PAGE → 28

Holyrood Park

Arthur's Seat

Meadow Park

Merchiston

Newington

Duddingston Loch

Prestonfield

1000 yd
1000 m

The map shows the location of the most interesting districts. There is a detailed map of each district on which each of the sights described is numbered.

Mr Hyde the murderer. In the end, you should leave the stage by the back door: to the west, you can then walk along the small river called the Water of Leith through a rustic idyll that runs down to the sea where the old port of Leith has now developed into a fashionable place to go out and have a good time.

OLD TOWN

The Royal Mile is where you will feel the real heartbeat and vivacity of Edinburgh all the way along its entire length of 5,900 feet – the equivalent of an old Scottish mile.

Strolling up and down the Mile, a day will pass in no time; it slopes slightly to the east all the way from the castle to the Palace of Holyroodhouse. Between the two, shops in the medieval "high-rises" do all they can to lure the crowds of tourists passing by with kilts, tartans and whisky. But you will also discover small basement restaurants and cafés, churches, museums and lanes with steps that branch off the Mile like ribs from the backbone. To the south, the streets appear more like canyons between the listed buildings. Small, steep connecting lanes such as *Victoria Street*, *Candlemaker Row* and *King's Stables Road* lead like arteries into the lively, beating heart of the Old Town. There, any number of boutiques flourish between tap rooms, coffee-houses and restaurants. And a pulsating nightlife can be found in the medieval labyrinth of streets between *Grassmarket, Cowgate* and *Nicholson Street*.

■ ARTHUR'S SEAT ☼
(115 F4) (*Ω J6*)

On a clear day, you can see more than 60 miles from the top of the most dramatic of the three volcanic hills in the city at a height of 823 ft. The volcanic stone block rises up like a rampart to the south of Holyroodhouse and the Scottish Parliament Building. A steep path leads you along the craggy Salisbury Crags to the top. After around 320 ft, you will already have a fine view of the Parliament and it is only from this perspective that you will be able to fully appreciate how it was slotted into the old city. If you intend to make the five-mile loop hike of the heights, you should be sure to wear sturdy shoes and weatherproof clothing. You might be caught out by the quickly changing weather and the rough terrain.

■ CAMERA OBSCURA ☼
(113 F2) (*Ω E5*)

It fascinated Victorian tourists from 1853 on and still attracts many visitors today. A kind of pinhole camera with a focal length of 337.7 inches projects views of Edinburgh in the dark upper storey of a tower next to the castle. As if by magic, images of sections of the city with the gentle charm of old drawings appear before the visitors' eyes in the tower room. The exhibitions you see on the way upstairs explain the context of the photographs. Modern telescopes have been set up on the roof of the Camera Obscura Tower to enable you to draw the New and Old Towns up close. Interactive exhibitions on six floors explain visual phenomena such as holograms and plasma-energy. The Camera Obscura is more interesting when the weather is fine but the exhibitions will also help you forget a rainy day. *Daily April–June 9:30am–8pm, July/Aug 9am–10pm, Sept/Oct 9:30am–8pm, Nov–March 10am–7pm | admission £15 | 549 Castlehill | www.camera-obscura.co.uk*

■3 EDINBURGH CASTLE ★ ● ☼
(113 E–F 2–3) (*ⅅ D–E5*)

This castle is the highlight of any city tour and one you will really have to look up to; not because of its physical appearance but because of its position on one of the three volcanic hills in the centre of the city. Castle Hill slopes steeply downwards on three sides but the Old Town finds its way gently into the valley on its eastern flank.

Heating like the knights of old in Edinburgh Castle

SIGHTSEEING IN OLD TOWN

■1 Arthur's Seat
■2 Camera Obscura
■3 Edinburgh Castle
■4 Greyfriars Kirkyard
■5 John Knox House

It is difficult to imagine just how remote this castle must have looked in the 7th century when King Edwin of Northumbria in the north-east of England had this lonely fortress erected here. Later, kings were fathered and born here, prisoners locked in the dungeons and guests assassinated.

The two freedom fighters William Wallace (1270–1305) and King Robert the Bruce (1274–1329) have taken up position at the entrance, the *Gatehouse* built in 1887. In summer, you will hardly be

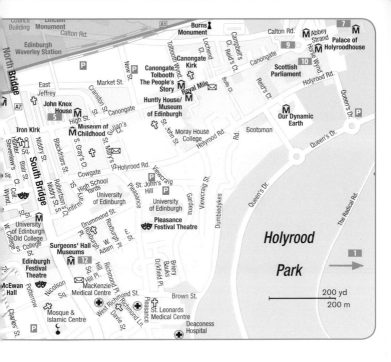

able to get a good look at them; there will be so many other visitors behind you pushing to get in.

Shortly after passing the bottleneck at the *Portcullis Gate*, you will find yourself standing in front of the two main attractions inside the castle: one of them is the enormous *Mons Meg Cannon* – probably produced in Mons in Belgium in 1457, it weighs 6 tons and could shoot stone cannonballs with a diameter of 20 inches weighing 150 kg. It was fired for the last time in 1681. Today, a modern 4.1 inch weapon lets off a shot everyday – except Sunday – at 1pm, a lot of people working down below in the city call this the "lunchtime bang". Be sure to cover your ears if you are there when it goes off! In the 19th century, sailors in the port outside the city used this to adjust their chronometers, so the shot could never be too loud.

The other highlight is *St Margaret's Chapel* from the 12th century. It was possibly built by King David I; in memory of his mother Margaret, a Scottish queen who was canonised for her social commitment. The elegant, unpretentious chapel with the slightly asymmetrical layout still has a touching effect on today's visitors, even though the interior has unfortunately been whitewashed.

The Scottish crown jewels (16th century) – the crown, created by James Mossmann (*John Knox House,* see p. 33), the sceptre and sword – are on display in the Crown Hall under the title *Honours of Scotland*. In 1996, they were joined by an even older – and, for Scots, much more important – ancient artefact, the *Stone of Scone.* The early kings of the Scots and Picts were crowned on this stone until the English seized it in 1296 and placed it under the English Coronation Chair. The then British Prime Minister John Major returned it 700 years later during a festive ceremony shortly before Scotland voted in favour of autonomy.

The rest of the castle is made up of a few barracks buildings but what's truly impressive is the view over the city and surrounding countryside. *Daily April–Sept 9:30am–6pm, Oct–March 9:30am–5pm | admission £17 | Castlehill | www.edinburghcastle.gov.uk*

4 ▪ GREYFRIARS KIRKYARD ●
(114 A3) (*F6*)

It doesn't get more uncanny or touching than this! The cemetery has grown dear to the hearts of the living as it is haunted with the ghosts of many stories. One of the most unusual attractions is the small monument to a Skye terrier which guarded his master's grave for 14 years after his burial until he finally died himself. He wasn't allowed to be buried on the spot, but has been commemorated since 1872 with this statue. The first church built after the Reformation is full of creepy charm. 1,200 radical Presbyterians, called Covenanters, who were against the Anglican version of the reformed church imposed by the English king, were forcibly detained here in the middle of the 17th century and many died. The stories you will hear on the unavoidable horror tours are even more dreadful. Burke and Hare were two body snatchers who dug up the corpses required by the Anatomic Institute for exploratory dissection. The two Irishmen became greedy and began to murder, and were finally found out when one of the corpses was recognised during an operation. The end of the story: Burke was hanged in front of 25,000 people, Hare

HEART OF MIDLOTHIAN

A large mosaic heart in the tarmac near the west portal of St Giles Cathedral and not far from the former parliament – today, a law court – can easily go unnoticed. But every resident of Edinburgh knows it and some still spit on it, as has been customary since the 15th century. This used to be the site of a prison and decapitated heads were displayed on spikes here. The locals used to protest by spitting in front of the prison gate. Walter Scott mentioned the gruesome prison in his novel *The Heart of Midlothian* (1818) and this is somewhat to blame for all the spitting! One of Edinburgh's football clubs is named after the novel's title and so fans of the local rival team, the Hibernians, also spit on the heart. *High Street/Royal Mile*

He wasn't as fragile in real life: a glass window with a picture of John Knox

saved himself as a chief witness. Less creepy and more reflective are the ● classical music concerts in the *Greyfriars Kirk*. *Mon–Fri 10:30am–4:30pm, Sat 11am 2pm | Greyfriars Place | Candlemaker Row/ Chambers Street | www.greyfriarskirk.com*

5 JOHN KNOX HOUSE ●
(114 B2) (*📖 G5*)

This 500-year-old historic house is definitely the most visually attractive building on the Royal Mile. John Knox, the founder of Scottish Presbyterianism, may possibly have lived in the building and this saved it from being demolished in 1830. It is certain, however, that the rich goldsmith James Mossmann, who was also responsible for the Scottish crown, actually did live here. He safeguarded his home by having an entrance on the first floor, stairs that are difficult to negotiate and false locks. His contemporary, Knox, was inspired by the religious reformer John Calvin in Geneva and set out to reform Scotland's church.

You enter the rooms where the faded original ceiling paintings and some furniture from the Knox and Mossmann era give an authentic atmosphere, via a spiral staircase. While you look out of the window at what is happening on the Royal Mile, you will suddenly hear debates Knox had with Mossmann and Mary Queen of Scots. The Catholic Queen of Scotland, who had been educated in France, and the strict, quarrelsome religious teacher often clashed with each other, particularly over her loose lifestyle. However, it should be mentioned that the democratic church reformer and father of several daughters was generally suspicious of woman, as shown in his treatise "The First Blast of the Trumpet against the Monstrous Regiment of Women," which is on display.

At the time, John Knox was considered an unusually eloquent speaker. The *Scottish Storytelling Centre* attached to John Knox House furthers rhetoric and the widespread Scottish pleasure in the art of telling tales. There is an interactive

"Scotland's Stories" exhibition in the cheerful rooms with the pleasant café. There are INSIDERTIP storytelling events *(from £5)* in the evening in a small theatre, in October the International Storytelling Festival is held. This is a good introduction to literary Edinburgh and Scotland. *Mon–Sat 10am–6pm, July, Aug also Sun noon–6pm | admission £5; Storytelling Centre: free | 43 High Street | Royal Mile | www.tracscotland.org*

🔲 NATIONAL MUSEUM OF SCOTLAND
(114 A–B3) (*ΩΩ F6*)

This is Scotland! Here, in magnificently grand halls, you will be served everything that makes the country stand out and all that it has gifted to the world. In the atrium in particular, Victorian royal grandeur is sublimely paired with ultra-modern museum architecture – a curious contrast to the spooky-mossy ambiance of the Greyfriars Cemetery next door. Inside, Scotland presents itself in all its facets: the blade from Edinburgh's guillotine, illuminating information on Dolly the genetically manipulated sheep that was cloned just six miles away in Roslin, stuffed animals and skeletons, minimalist fashion creations designed by Jean Muir, who died in 1995 – she had Scottish parents – and the supposed relics of St Columba, the Irish-Celtic monk who converted the Scottish Picts to Christianity in the 6th century, along with many objects from the world of technology, decorative art, design, fashion and science. A hybrid museum that never ceases to amaze its visitors. After the visit, you can fortify yourself in 🔆 *The Tower (daily noon–11pm | tel. 0131 225 30 03 | www.tower-restaurant.com | Moderate)* restaurant in the new building – stylish ambience, good choice of vegetarian dishes, wheelchair accessible. INSIDERTIP Great view of the Old Town and the castle accompanied by a glass of wine. *Daily 10am–5pm | free*

The country in all its facets: National Museum of Scotland

admission | Chambers Street/Candle-maker Row | www.nms.ac.uk

7 PALACE OF HOLYROODHOUSE
(111 D–E 5–6) (*ID H4*)

The Royal Mile becomes really regal at the bottom. Seeing that there is (currently) no Scottish king, the English monarch has to come by once a year to air the palace. Without that, Holyroodhouse – which looks more like a stately home than a palace – would possibly once again fall into the poor state it was in when the young composer Felix Mendelssohn-Bartholdy saw it in 1829: dilapidated, without a roof, overgrown with ivy. The musician stated that this had inspired him to the somewhat lugubrious oboe melody at the beginning of his romantic "Scottish Symphony". It might be a good idea to listen to the work on your MP-3 player instead of the voice on the audio-guide when you make your way through the dozen or so rooms that can be visited. Some bedrooms and dining rooms are open to the public if the Queen is not in town. As with the castle, Holyroodhouse's history is what makes it really fascinating. When King David I was threatened with being horned by a stag while hunting, he had a vision of the Holy Cross between the animal's antlers and his tragic fate was warded off. After this, the King had the Augustine Order build a monastery to the Holy Cross (*Holy Rood*); its ruins next to the palace invite visitors to take a stroll. A visit to the palace is an absolute must for fans of historical conspiracy theories – this is where Mary Stuart's Italian secretary David Rizzio was murdered in front of the pregnant Queen. The Catholic Mary Stewart, who had spent her youth in France and gallicised the name into Stuart, returned to an austere, Calvinist Edinburgh where she married her cousin Lord Darnley. He – as well as the Presbyterian clique of the nobility – found his wife's predilection for literature and singing not particularly Scottish. Rizzio the aesthete had to be done away with. Darnley himself was assassinated a little later; but that is not part of the palace's history.

The fascinating mixture of the Scottish baronial style and elements of a French château develops a INSIDER TIP special charm in the evening when the setting sun lights up the palace's main façade. The rooms in the adjacent *Queen's Gallery* show changing exhibitions from the Royal Collection in Windsor Castle. *April–Oct daily 9:30am–6pm, Nov–March 9:30am–4:30pm | admission £11.30; £14 with Queen's Gallery | Canongate | The Royal Mile | www.royalcollection.org.uk*

8 THE REAL MARY KING'S CLOSE ●
(110 A6) (*ID F5*)

The former labyrinth of small streets next to the Royal Mile was re-built in 2003 and was re-opened as an exciting tourist attraction. Its reputation as a haunted close originated from the hallucinating, eerie gases which escaped into the close from the stagnant and highly polluted marsh Nor Loch nearby – today Princes Street Gardens; this was intensified by the stories of hauntings of plague victims quarantined in the close. A visit to the close (online booking strongly recommended) lets you explore the medieval hauntings in Edinburgh. *Mid-March–Oct daily 10am–9pm, Nov–Mid-March Sun–Thu 10am–5pm, Fri, Sat 10am–9pm | admission £15.50 | 2 Warriston's Close/High Street | www.realmarykingsclose.com*

9 ROYAL MILE ★
(114–115 A–D 2–1) (*ID E–H 4–5*)

It is said that around 50,000 people lived on the Royal Mile and the streets branching off of it – the so-called *closes* and *wynds* – in the 18th century; the highest population density in Europe at the time. The residential buildings, the *lands*, had as many as 16 storeys; the simple folk lived at the bottom and top while the better-off merchants and craftsmen had their flats in between. The well-trodden steps on the left and right of the Mile can lead to picturesque courtyards – it is worth following them from time to time. Or you might unexpectedly topple over the threshold of a hidden pub and soon get into a chat with the locals at the bar over a lukewarm glass of top-fermented ale. Keep an eye open for guided ghost

LOW BUDGET

A *Ridacard (lothianbuses.com/tickets/ridacard)* entitles you to unlimited travel on all Lothian bus services and trams. The card is worth buying if you're staying a week in Edinburgh and costs £19.

Admission to the national museums is free! This also applies to the *Royal Botanic Garden* and the ● *Tartan Weaving Mill & Exhibition (daily 9am–5:30pm | 555 Castlehill | Royal)*, a kilt factory that shows all stages in the production of the multi-coloured cloth, from shearing the sheep to trying on the finished garment.

There is no need to take a taxi back to your hotel after midnight – you can use one of the *Night Buses*. The eleven lines are marked with an "N" at most bus stops and some of them even travel as far as ten miles out of town *(night fare £3 | lothian buses.com)*.

and street-ballad tours. Thank goodness, he ultimate horror has been done away with: today, nobody has to take cover when the bell of St Giles chimes 10 o'clock – followed by the warning cry of *"gardy luh"* (from the French "gardez l'eau" – watch out, water!) – when the contents of all the chamber pots were emptied into the streets.

The Royal Mile is roughly divided into four sections: *Castle Hill, Lawnmarket, High Street* and *Canongate*. Lawnmarket boasts a monument to the famous Edinburgh philosopher and economist David Hume (1711–76), a friend of the economist and philosopher Adam Smith. ● *Free tours* through the city start at 11am, 1pm and 3pm from *Tron Kirk* in the High Street *(www.newedinburghtours. eu)*, meeting point in front of Starbuck's. Especially in the upper half, the Mile is a succession of little shops stuffed with Scotch kitsch. The centrepiece is the main church, *St Giles Cathedral*, with its walk-in roof.

For many years, Canongate lay outside the city boundary separated by the *Flodden Wall*; you can still see traces of this in the tarmac on the street between Greyfriars and the National Museum *(corner of Chambers Street/Forrest Road)*. There is a statue of the talented poet Robert Fergusson (1750–74) in front of the small *Canongate Kirk* in the Canongate section (the Queen and other members of the Royal Family often attend services here when they are at the palace). When the life-sized statue of the vigorously striding poet done by sculptor Robert Anand in 2004 was unveiled in front of thousands of spectators not far away from the parliament, an actor dressed up as Robert Burns leaped out of the crowd and recited some of Fergusson's verses. You will also find traces of Fergusson in *Canongate Ceme-*

tery, where he is buried, as are Adam Smith and Mary Stuart's murdered secretary David Rizzio. Robert Burns, who was born nine years after Fergusson, was greatly inspired by the young genius and donated his gravestone.

2004 and could no longer explain one of the puzzling features of the Parliament; namely, the scale-like design of the rear windows.

There is a section where the astonishingly spacious building amalgamates with a

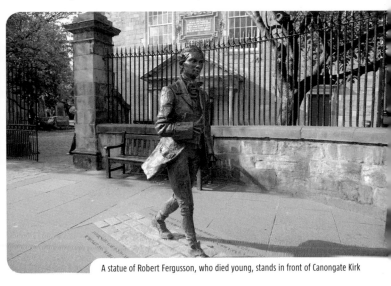

A statue of Robert Fergusson, who died young, stands in front of Canongate Kirk

10 SCOTTISH PARLIAMENT ★
(115 D1) (*ฬ H4–5*)

An exciting contrast in building styles awaits the visitor at the lower end of the Royal Mile. In Edinburgh, the Catalan architect Enric Miralles demonstrated how a modern building could find its place in the narrow sea of houses, many of which had been constructed centuries ago. Most people saw this as poetic architecture orientated on the geography of the Old Town and geology of Scotland while others complained that it was much too expensive. The international community acknowledges how utterly successful Miralles' building is. However, the architect died in 2000 at the young age of 45 before construction was completed in

house from 1685 *(Queensberry House)*, making it possible for a ghost living there to participate in the meetings of parliament held from Tueday to Thursday. On Wednesdays and Thursdays it is possible to attend the parliamentary meetings of the 129 MPs; free tickets for the *Public Gallery* can be ordered in advance and are much in demand *(tel. 0131 3 48 52 00 or 800 0 92 71 00)*. There is also a very interesting ● INSIDER TIP free one-hour tour *(11am, 1pm, 3pm | book online)* on days when there are no meetings. If you don't want to take part in this, information is provided in an exhibition and you can go to the café. *Mon, Fri, Sat 10am–5pm, Tue–Thu 9am–6:30pm | free admission | Canongate | www.parliament.scot*

11 ST GILES CATHEDRAL ●
(114 A2) (*ΩΩ F5*)

St Giles does not seem very inviting at first glance. The compact building is almost overpowered by the phalanx of tall buildings from the late Middle Ages on the Royal Mile and you could possibly even walk past it if it was not for the boldly playful tower crown. And this, even though the *High Kirk of St Giles* is the Mother Church of Scottish Presbyterianism. It is actually not even a cathedral seeing that St Giles was only an Anglican Episcopal See for two short periods in the 17th century. The Church of Scotland has a democratic assembly of Presbyters instead of a strict hierarchy.

Church services have been held here since 854 although the pillars around the altar from 1120 are now the oldest remains of the building to have survived. The new building was erected in the Gothic style after its predecessor had been destroyed by the English. The severe Gothic dimensions must have pleased John Knox: it provided the perfect stage for the blazing sermons he delivered from 1560 to 1572. St Giles hardly came to rest later on either. Edinburgh's church history is characterised by countless intellectual conflicts on the true faith and appropriate building.

The tour is well worth it. The fascinating INSIDER**TIP** ▶ *Chapel of the Scottish Order of the Thistle*, built in 1911, is a real gem with its exquisite wood and stone carving. The national emblem of Scotland in the Order's name – the second highest British honour after the Order of the Garter – is a clear indication as to why the majority of the 16 knights should be Scots. The Queen, as Sovereign, the Duke of Edinburgh, the Prince of Wales and the Princess Royal as extra knights and ladies, bring the number of members to 20. If necessary, the row of knights is made complete by royal appointment in November.

Each knight has his own seat decorated with his coat of arms – commoners have to have one designed before they can be admitted to the Order – in the oak stalls. David Steel, the first president of the Scottish parliament, had a jaguar added to his metal shield; some people feel that he did this because he was so fond of the car with this name. King Olav of Norway was admitted as an extra member. The most peculiar decorations in the chapel are two angels playing bagpipes. INSIDER**TIP** ▶ A 20-minute guided tour on the church's roof (£6) offers an unusual view. *May–Sept Mon–Fri 9am–7pm, Sat 9am–5pm, Sun 1pm–5pm, Oct–April*

TIME TO CHILL

There are several exquisite feelgood oases in the city, the best being the
● *One Spa (daily from 8am, swimming from 6:30am | 3 hours £70 (swimming, gym, sauna, relax) | 8 Conference Square | www.onespa.com)* on the roof of the 5-star hotel *Sheraton Grand*: world-class offers including Turkish bath, aroma grottoes, massages and

ergonomic loungers, exercise machines, rainforest-scented showers and a salt-water outdoor pool with a view over the city.

You can also visit the spa areas of the Grandhotel *Balmoral* (see p. 78) – and afterwards rave about the wonderful experience at the whisky bar or in the excellent restaurant.

Mon–Sat 9am–5pm, Sun 1pm–5pm | free admission | Lawnmarket, Royal Mile

NEW TOWN

12 SURGEONS' HALL MUSEUM
(114 B3) (𝄐 G6)

Liver, lungs, lymph – how are the organs, skeleton and nervous system all interconnected? The famous museum gets right under the skin, to the places you normally can't see without X-ray eyes. This temple of the body cult has been a dissection theatre for surgeons and pathologists since 1832. Everything behind the columned entrance was revamped in 2015 and the old operation theatre was even furnished with a INSIDER TIP digital cadaver – explore every corner of the anatomy with a swipe of your hand. Interactivity is complemented by astonishing exhibits and ironic creepiness, when you stumble upon a notebook said to be made of the skin of the grave robber William Burke. And find out how doctor and author Arthur Conan Doyle wrote the role of Sherlock Holmes' crony Dr Watson here and pioneered the use of fingerprinting as forensic evidence. *Daily 10am–5pm| admission £6.50 | Nicolson Street | museum.rcsed.ac.uk*

13 THE WRITERS' MUSEUM ●
(114 A2) (𝄐 E5)

This building from 1622 is the only original house in the street leading off of the Lawnmarket section of the Royal Mile. Today, it is a museum commemorating the writer trio Burns, Scott and Stevenson. Early editions of their works are on display along with personal mementos including Burns' snuffbox. There is also a INSIDER TIP very cosy corner where you can settle down for a good read. Sometimes even modern authors are given exhibitions. *Wed–Sat 10am–5pm, in Aug also Sun noon–5pm | free admission | Lady Stair's Close | Lawnmarket, Royal Mile*

The New Town could be described as Edinburgh's "better half" where visitors no longer have to find their way through the narrow canyons of the Old Town, but can stroll at ease through a generous, bright rectangle of streets with uniform three-storey façades that was laid 200 years ago.

Entrance to the world of literature: The Writers' Museum

One regularly repeated architectural element is the semicircular fanlight over front doors. And rows of house façades and terraced town houses from the time when all of the kings were called George. Three long, main streets highlight the east-west axis. *George Street*, named after George III, dominates the scene from the ridge of a hill and seems to be the Georgian answer to the medieval Royal Mile. There are many top international – and especially London-based – fashion stores, café and nightclubs behind the large windows and in the basements.

Shopping and window-shopping is a very relaxed affair here. It is interesting that

INSIDER TIP Sunday is the most pleasant day to go for a stroll or shop anywhere in the New Town; this is when even Edinburgh's bankers and other workers unwind a bit and go to cafés for a chat and to read their *Scotland on Sunday* newspaper.

The life of Scotland's capital pulsates on Princes Street

SIGHTSEEING IN NEW TOWN

1 Calton Hill
2 Charlotte Square
3 Georgian House

A highlight of new elegance in old town houses can be seen on the recently renovated *St Andrew Square* with every shopper's paradise, Harvey Nichols, at its east end. Further to the east, *St James Centre*, a shopping centre and office block built in the 1960s, shows what can happen when the good taste of the Georgian period of around 1800 is ignored. It is currently undergoing a facelift – an ultra-modern, multifunctional shopping centre will open here in 2020. The heart of the New Town is bordered by *Princes Street* and *Queen Street* on both sides of George Street. The two, somewhat narrower,

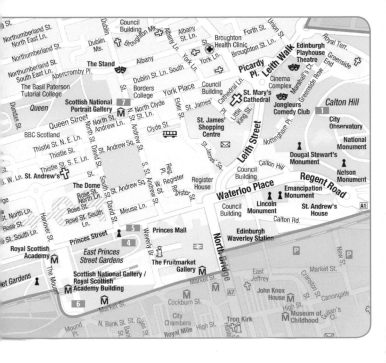

4 Princes Street Gardens
5 Scott Monument
6 Scottish National Gallery

7 Scottish National Portrait Gallery

Pedestrian zone

Thistle and *Rose Streets,* named after the national flowers of Scotland and England, with their many inexpensive shops and pubs lie like mirror images between the three main streets. From the north-south axes that cross George Street at regular intervals, you look towards the Old Town on the one side, and the Firth of Forth inlet on the other. The New Town stretches northwards from Queen Street as far as *Fettes College,* Edinburgh's Eton. The circular Georgian residential streets *Royal Circus, Moray Place* and *Ainslie Place* are three of the pearls in the crown of the New Town.

■ CALTON HILL ★ ● ☀
(110 C4–5) (*∅ G3–4*)

Shortly before sunset, photographers haul their tripods up the hill, couples have cheese and wine – or even champagne – in their rucksacks. This is the **INSIDER TIP** best place in town to enjoy the twilight hour. Balmoral Hotel and the castle are illuminated focal points; the traffic on Princes Street draws a line of light towards the west. The silhouette of the Old Town in front of Arthur's Seat dominates the view to the left and, to the right, the eye swings towards the port and Firth of Forth.

This is a view one cannot get enough of but it is also a strange kind of architectonic rendezvous, for the area on the park-like hill is taken up by a disparate group of monuments that appear to have been placed here due to lack of space somewhere else. The twelve Doric columns designed by Edinburgh's Neoclassicist builder William Henry Playfair were erected in 1822 as a *National Monument*. It was planned to be a bombastic war memorial but the necessary funding ran out; today this reminder of a Greek temple still touches the soul of any romantic person gazing up at it on the eastern horizon from Princes Street.

Next to it, the 105 ft high tower of the ☆ *Nelson Monument (April–Sept Mon–Sat 1–7pm, Oct–March Mon–Sat 10am–4pm | admission free, admission tower: £5)* from the same period rises. 143 steps lead up to the most magnificent view of the city – a delight when there is not a strong wind. It is 4,000 ft as the crow flies to the castle and that is exactly the length of the steel cable that was stretched between the huge clock on the tower and the castle in 1861. It was intended to fire a cannon shot at exactly 1pm every day – as a signal for sailors in the port of Leith who could not see the clock tower when it was foggy.

The monumental duo is complemented by Playfair's stocky *City Observatory*, as well as his small memorial temple – another Greek inspiration – for the Edinburgh moral philosopher Dugald Stewart (1753–1828) and a monument to the local mathematician John Playfair (1748–1819). Further down the hill take a stroll through INSIDER TIP *Calton Cemetery* and past the grand terrace houses designed by Playfair that run along the eastern contour of the hill.

2 CHARLOTTE SQUARE ★
(113 D1–2) (*ϕ D4–5*)

This rectangle surrounded by elegant façades at the west end of the New Town is the top address in Edinburgh – from a political point of view. The *Secretary of State for Scotland* resided in *house no. 6* until 1999. Today, it is the home of the head of the Scottish government and brings a touch of London's 10 Downing Street to Edinburgh. As you walk past, you will get a feeling for the political and lobbying business in Edinburgh. However, the First Minister's home is no different from the other houses including the *Georgian House (no. 7)* that is now a museum. Many famous people had Charlotte Square as their address; these include the inventor of the telephone Alexander Graham Bell,

FIT IN THE CITY

Just walking up and down the steps and steep streets of the Old Town should take care of average fitness requirements. The sloping profile of the city offers many interesting places for runners: an early-morning run through the still deserted *Princes Street Gardens* below the castle is a wonderful experience. Beautiful landscape can be enjoyed on runs along the *Water of Leith* and up to Arthur's Seat from the lower end of Royal Mile. A network of eleven routes along former railway tracks covers a distance of 47 miles outside the road network. Maps are available to find your way around *(www.innertubemap.com)*.

the founder of hospital hygiene Joseph Lister, as well as Field Marshal Douglas Haig, British Commander-in-Chief on the Western Front in World War I.

3 ■ GEORGIAN HOUSE
(113 D1) (*D4*)

This is the perfect place to find out about life in an upper-class Georgian home in Edinburgh. Form the outside, house no. 7 is a typical terrace house at the northern end of Charlotte Square with a (Neo) classicist, symmetrical façade in the style propagated by the architect Robert Adams. The uniformity of the layout continues on the inside where it also contrasts with the fascinating, cosy interior. Georgian taste could not tolerate any carpets on the floor, in contrast to the later more pompous Victorian period. The kitchen and dining room are real eye-catchers and you will probably immediately feel you would like to sit down at the table. The charming National Trust stewards know how to stop that but they

will let you in on the most intimate secrets of the high society between 1714 and 1837. *Daily March-Oct 10am–5pm, Nov–Dec 11am–4pm, April–June, Sept, Oct 10am–5pm, July, Aug 10am–7pm | admission £8 | 7 Charlotte Square | www. nts.org.uk*

4 ■ PRINCES STREET GARDENS ★ ●
(113–114 E–A 2–1) (*D–F 5–4*)

The Gardens are Edinburgh's "green lungs", the city's "solarium" and a place where events are held. They were laid out when the New Town was being built around 1800 and a long narrow lake, where supposedly witches and rubbish were disposed of, was drained. The park landscape that came into being stretches along the south side of the entire length of Princes Street, which was not built up on the park side so as not to obstruct the view of the skyline of the Old Town. The *East Gardens* are dominated by the Scott Monument and continue to *Waverley Station* – the main railway station

Edinburgh's Central Park: Princes Street Gardens

named after a series of novels by Walter Scott – and the *Fruit Market Gallery*. By the way, the **INSIDER TIP** large clock on the tower of the palace-like Balmoral Hotel is two minutes fast to prevent passengers from missing their trains. Only on New Year's Eve is the correct time shown. A train leaves Waverley every fifteen minutes for Glasgow and the charming waiting room is also worth taking a look at. In December, a well-stocked Christmas Market is held behind the Scott Monument and an ice-skating rink is also opened. On the southern end of the station, the *Dungeons* chamber of horrors *(Nov–April daily 11am–4pm, April–19 July daily 10am–5pm, 20 July–31 Aug daily 10am–7pm, 1 Sept–31 Oct daily 10am–5pm | admission £16.20, online pre-booking £10.95 | 32 Market Street | www.thedungeons.com/edin*

burgh) is a cavern full of combative figures; something for the intrepid with a fondness for trivial action.

A steep street, *The Mound*, divides the park and leads up to the Old Town; on the way, the temple-like architecture of the *Royal Scottish Academy* and *Scottish National Gallery* will possibly make you slow down a bit and stride past them ceremoniously. There is a **INSIDER TIP** relief at the foot of a flight of steps that provides a good 3-dimensional overview of Edinburgh's geography. The ☼ *West Gardens* are a wonderful place for a stroll, a climb up to the castle or for simply enjoying the view. This is also a very popular meeting place for locals. In summer, the aroma of coffee wafts out of the *Open Air Café*, water bubbles in a fountain, floral arrangements add touches of colour and the fair-skinned Scots of the capital city attempt to get a

Unbelievably beautiful: the stained-glass works of art in St John's

bit of colour. The people of Edinburgh love their popular park on the slope and have a great time there. This is the stage for the loudest music and festival events in the city and there is an especially festive atmosphere in the evening when one gazes up at the illuminated castle.

Things become a bit less profane and more picturesquely spooky at the western end of Princes Street Gardens. This is where *St Cuthbert's Churchyard* connects with not one but two churches: *St Cuthbert's Kirk (5 Lothian Road | www.st-cuthberts.net)* is a stately, roundish basilica in the midst of the green of the trees with an interior decorated in warm tones. *St John's (3 Lothian Road | www.stjohnsedinburgh.org.uk)* on the other hand is an overpowering Victorian barrage constructed in the late-Gothic Perpendicular style and decorated with the most exquisite church windows in town. Especially in winter, the gravestones in the cemetery provide a INSIDER TIP fabulous foreground for photos of the castle when there are no leaves on the trees to block the view. *Princes Street*

5 ■ SCOTT MONUMENT
(114 A1) (*DD E5*)

The writer's monument to end all writer's monuments is located on Princes Street. After climbing up the 287 steps at several levels you will be able to look down on the city. In summer, there are long queues of people at the entrance and the narrow staircase means that some of them will still not have managed to get out again after an hour.

When Walter Scott died in 1832, the decision was made to create a dramatic monument in his memory. There was a neo-Gothic spirit at this time of transition from the sober Georgian to the ostentatious Victorian style. This means that Scott was presented with an ornate Gothic tower made of sandstone housing 64 figures from the writer's novels and 16 portrait busts of other Scottish poets. Today, the 200 ft high construction stands there like the spire of a church tower without a base. A quarry had to be reopened when renovation work was carried out in 1998/99 but the colour of the delicate sandstone has suffered – partly as a result of traffic pollution. *April–Sept daily 10am–7pm, Oct–March Mon–Sat 10am–4pm | admission £5 | East Princes Street Gardens*

6 ■ SCOTTISH NATIONAL GALLERY ●
(114 A2) (*DD E4–5*)

The National Gallery is enveloped with the aura of a meeting place from Greek antiquity, partly due to the neo-classical columned façade of the two main buildings. You don't even have to go inside – just enjoy the atmosphere created by self-appointed orators and chattering little groups. Eventually the incessant sound of bagpipes will force you inside after all. Here you will relish, for free (!), countless paintings by old masters, impressionists and expressionists as well as important Scottish painters, all hung closely together. The *Royal Scottish Academy Building (www.royalscottishacademy.org)*, where you will be asked to pay for special exhibitions, also belongs to the National Gallery.

A third modern wing connects the 19th-century temples and offers sanctuary in its café. A certain kind of cult has developed around the small portrait of *The Reverend Robert Walker Skating on Duddingston Loch*, painted by the high-society artist Henry Raeburn in 1795. It shows Walker, the vicar of Canongate Church and a member of the honourable *Edinburgh Skating Society* on the ice, in a comically stiff pose balancing on one leg and wearing a forbidding black frock

Edinburgh reveals its rural side in Stockbridge, on the opposite banks of the Water of Leith

coat and top hat. INSIDER TIP ▶ Delicate watercolours by William Turner are displayed every January when the winter light can do them the least damage. *Daily 10am–5pm, Thu 10am–7pm | free admission | 72 The Mound | www. nationalgalleries.org*

7 SCOTTISH NATIONAL PORTRAIT GALLERY (110 A5) (*∅ F4*)

This is where you can find the "who's who" of Scottish society captured in every kind of portrait imaginable: an exhibition of Scottish heroes from Sean Connery or the author Irvine Welsh and football trainer Alex Ferguson to Bonnie Prince Charlie and – of course – Mary Stuart. This is complemented by an outstandig collection of photography. The entrance hall itself is a real eye-catcher. INSIDER TIP ▶ A must: the contemporary gallery and the wonderful café. *1 Queen Street | www.nationalgalleries.org*

MORE SIGHTS

Edinburgh exudes rural charm in Dean Village and Stockbridge to the west and northwest of the heart of the city.

The small river known as the Water of Leith creates a natural border between the elegant façades of the New Town and residential roads, hidden houses and suburban streets of shops such as *Raeburn Place*. Explore some of the small boutiques and rub shoulders with the locals at the bar. Linger for a while on the small bridges over the river and in front of carefully restored buildings from the industrial age in *Dean Village*. And if you have the stamina and the right shoes, follow

the idyllic course of the river as far as *Leith*, where the out-of-town port has developed into a place for gourmets and night-owls to enjoy themselves. If you keep going as far as the beach at *Portobello*, you will have completed an arc from the west to north-east around the centre of the capital city.

CRAMOND ISLE (116 C1) *(∅ 0)*

A walk on the wild side! A spot of wilderness in the suburbs, one mile offshore in the Firth of Forth, beckons you to take part in a balancing act in the play of the tides. The little island is half way between Leith and the Forth Bridges. It is best to only take the walk two hours either side of low tide, otherwise you'll be stuck over there for six hours. The causeway is lined with antitank concrete teeth, making the trip even more bizarre.

Drink a toast to your trip out to sea with a pint in the rustic *Cramond Inn (Moderate)*. Bus 41

INSIDER TIP ▶ PORTOBELLO
(117 D1) *(∅ 0)*

Its claim to be the "Brighton of the North" is definitely a bit exaggerated. But the large sandy beach only about 30 minutes by bus from Princes Street is very popular on hot summer days. The long promenade, the typical, nostalgic Victorian seaside charm, cafés, pubs, ice cream and chips, and the curious middle-class houses in the streets behind the beach make an excursion here well worth it. In winter, it is the perfect place for a melancholic stroll along the seashore as far as the newly designed port district of Leith. Bus 26

ROYAL BOTANIC GARDEN ★
(109 D–E 1–2) *(∅ C–D 1–2)*

Scotland is famous for its magnificent landscaped gardens and the Royal Botanic Garden is the epitome of floral glory. The complex is 200 years old, somewhat younger than London's Kew Gardens, but it is also an important research site. With its rock and Chinese gardens, pavilions and wonderful, recently renovated glasshouses, it is the INSIDER TIP ▶ only tropical location in Edinburgh. It also has the oldest collections of botanical literature in Great Britain. You will need some extra time to visit the shop and café terrace. The view of the medieval skyline of the city from the ⚘ *Terrace Café* is a real delight *(March–Sept daily 10am–5:30pm | tel. 0131 5 52 06 16 | Budget)*. Nov–Jan daily 10am–4pm, Feb, Oct 10am–5pm, March–Sept 10am–6pm | admission: glasshouses £6.50, children under 15: free; garden: free | Arboretum Place | Stockbridge | www.rbge.org.uk | buses 23, 27

ROYAL YACHT BRITANNIA ★ ●
(115 E1) (*M K1*)

Her Majesty set out to sea in this Art Deco yacht from 1953 to 1997; she visited and played hostess to illustrious statesmen, royals and even Gandhi. The yacht is decorated in a style typical of the taste of post-war Britain. The audio-guide will help you place certain figures in the right context.

Visitors go on board the queen-sized yacht in the port of Leith through the *Ocean Terminal* (with its own shopping centre) planned by the star designer Terence Conran. *Jan–March, Nov, Dec daily 10am–3:30pm, April, May, June, Oct daily 9am–4:30pm, July–Sept 9:30am–4:30pm | admission £15.50 | Ocean Drive | Leith | www.royalyachtbritannia.org.uk | buses 11, 13, 34, 300*

SCOTTISH NATIONAL GALLERY OF MODERN ART ONE ★
(112 A2) (*M A5*)

What is possibly the best art museum in town is located in the rural surround-ings of Dean Village – go inside, even though you might have had enough of Neoclassicist sandstone buildings. The international artistic universe of the past hundred years is represented here – from Matisse to Hockney and Pollock, alongside various modern Scottish art movements. The café is wonderful and is well worth a visit not only for its tasty snacks made with fresh local products – the same applies to Charles Jencks' landscape sculpture.

The ● *Scottish National Gallery of Modern Art Two* (112 B1) (*M B4*) opposite is more intimate. The exhibitions are dominated by Surrealism and Dadaism and there is also a replica of the studio where Eduardo Paolozzi (1924–2005), Edinburgh's greatest modern artist, once worked. Recommended: A visit to the nice café. *Daily 10am–5pm | free admission | 75 Belford Road | www.national galleries.org | bus 41*

A museum visit can ideally be combined with a stroll along the river *Water of Leith* (see p. 42).

FOR BOOKWORMS & FILM BUFFS

Doors Open – A thriller by Ian Rankin (2008) without the solitary Inspector Rebus about an ingenious theft of a painting in Edinburgh

Trainspotting – Notoriously famous novel (1993) by Irvine Welsh that digs deep into the life of drug addicts in Leith. Welsh cut open Edinburgh's soul with his social scalpel. Director Danny Boyle served up impressive cinematic adaptations with the Scottish actors Ewan McGregor and Robert Carlyle in 1996 and 2017

Breaking the Waves – The 1996 film by Danish director Lars von Trier depicts the hopeless conflict of a young woman trapped in a Presbyterian Calvinist seaside community. Emily Watson stars in this melodrama set in barren Scottish landscape

The Angels' Share – Director Ken Loach descended into the Scottish petty-criminal milieu in 2012 to have uprooted youths break into a distillery to steal the most expensive whisky of all time

An excursion to Glasgow offers a contrast to tranquil Edinburgh

FURTHER AFIELD

GLASGOW (116 A2) (*m* 0)

Scotland's largest city with a population of 750,000 is only a fifty-minute train ride away from Waverley Station; there are four departures every hour. You will come across a glaring contrast to Edinburgh: post-industrial charm, rough slang, no-frills urbanity. Glasgow is more hectic than Edinburgh and not all homogenous. The unsophisticated but hearty charm of the city appeals to many visitors. Unlike the more refined residents of Edinburgh, the Glaswegians don't mince their words. As soon as you leave *Queen Street Station*, you will feel the tingling large-city atmosphere. 150 years ago, Glasgow was superior to London in almost all fields. You will get an idea of this when you cross *George Square* from the railway station to the Renaissance-style town hall, the *City Chambers*; Carrara marble was used for its extravagant interior around 1890. On the corner, the renovated post-industrial *Merchant City* – a magnet for shoppers, full of boutiques, art galleries, bars and restaurants – pulsates with life. A visit to the marvellous *Glasgow School of Art (www.gsa.ac.uk)* designed by the Art Nouveau genius Charles Rennie Mackintosh is an absolute must.

ROSSLYN CHAPEL (117 D2) (*m* 0)

Situated just six miles to the south of Edinburgh in the village of Roslin (where incidentally Dolly, the first cloned sheep, was born), this fascinating chapel is the subject of many myths and legends and appears in the novel "The Da Vinci Code" by Dan Brown. The "facts" about the Templar and the Holy Grail quoted in the novel have proved just as susceptible as the stonemasonry work exposed to 550 years of erosion. A visitor's centre provides explanations to the enigmatic stone carvings. *Mon–Sat 9.30am–5pm, So noon–4.45pm | admission £9 | Chapel Loan | www.rosslynchapel.org.uk | buses 37, 40 Roslin Hotel*

FOOD & DRINK

Edinburgh's restaurants are booming! The Scots have always placed great value on their Angus beef, fish from the rivers and the Atlantic, scallops and oysters. In the past years, a new creativity – mostly with its roots in France – has found its way into their preparation.

This revolution in the culinary art has really made itself felt in the pubs. Simple pub food, such as fish 'n' chips, lasagne and stew, have become much tastier. Gastro pubs have developed small, exquisite menus that have become just as important as the list of whiskies and different types of ale. They also use many local products such as pheasant and mussels and often mention where they come from. The setting also plays a major role. Since the mid 1990s, restaurants have opened in interesting, old buildings in the Old and New Towns. The former port of Leith has blossomed into Scotland's culinary centre; two of the chefs working there have been awarded at least one Michelin star. Cafés – usually open from 9am to 5pm or 6pm – are shooting up like mushrooms. But, in spite of all the changes, the new chefs do not ignore the old rustic hits from the local kitchen such as porridge, black pudding and haggis – however, today they are seasoned with more sophistication. Asian restaurants and continental cuisine round off Edinburgh's culinary scene.

Lunch is usually served from noon until 2pm and dinner from around 5pm to 11pm. Take-aways are open until 1am or 2am, if you are still hungry. Restaurants

Just fish and chips – you must be joking! Both pub food and haute cuisine have improved immensely in Edinburgh

and pubs have a good selection of wines. Others don't have a license and let you bring your own wine for a corkage fee *(BYOB – bring your own bottle | £1–3)*, others offer *BYOB* as an extra.

CAFÉS & CAFÉ RESTAURANTS

CAFÉ HUB
(114 A2) (*E5*)
This tower of a former neo-Gothic church is the *Hub* everything on the upper section of the Royal Mile revolves around. You

can buy tickets for the Edinburgh Festival here and it also has the best café terrace near the castle. *Daily | Castlehill | Old Town | tel. 0131 473 20 67 | www.thehub-edinburgh.com*

COLONNADES@THE SIGNET LIBRARY
● (118 A2) (*F5*)
This is the most elegant tearoom in Edinburgh in a spacious Georgian library hall. Fantastic New-Town feeling right in the Old Town. A hearty soup for lunch? Even better, book in advance and dive

CAFÉS & CAFÉ RESTAURANTS

into the full-blown tea time ceremony *(1–5pm, £32).* That's World Heritage atmosphere at its best. *Closed on Sat. | Parliament Square | Old Town | tel. 0131 2 26 10 64 | www.thesignetlibrary.co.uk/ colonnades*

the labyrinthine Old Town. Whether it's a simple snack with a glass of wine for lunch or duck breast for dinner – everything is tasty and finely prepared. *Daily | 6a Nicholson Street | Old Town | tel. 0131 6 23 17 52*

Man's best friend on the walls, delicious fish dishes on your plate: The Dogs

FALKO (113 D6) *(ℳ C8)*

If Edinburgh can attract a German master confectioner, the art of baking must really be on the up like a yeasty dough. Falko Burkert runs a wonderful café and bakery. It enjoys cult status – because he believes in taste over showiness, handicraft and a 100-year-old sourdough. *Wed–Sun | 185 Bruntsfield Place | South | tel. 0131 6 56 07 63 | www.falko.co.uk*

SPOON (114 B2) *(ℳ F5)*

A hint of the Rowling story. The first volume of "Harry Potter" was written here. The spacious retro style is a contrast to

THE CHOCOLATE TREE ● ◉
(113 D6) *(ℳ D8)*

Don't let them hear you say chocolate is unhealthy! This shop to the south of the Old Town offers chocolates made with ingredients from organic farms. It is cast in original shapes such as Venetian masks and ginger Buddhas. The makers are at the *Farmer's Market* (see p. 64) near the castle on Saturday. You can sample the delights at the small tables, or sign up for a INSIDER TIP 90-minute chocolate workshop *(on some Fridays, £20). Daily | 123 Bruntsfield Place | South tel. 0131 2 28 31 44 | www.choctree.co.uk*

VALVONA & CROLLA ⭐

The Italian delicatessen café with hams hanging from the ceiling, the aroma of coffee, cheese, pastries and freshly-baked bread in the air, is the result of a wave of Italian emigration more than 100 years ago. Enter the magical world of delicious breakfast and first-rate luncheon creations in the parent shop in Broughton *(110 C4) (𝄞 G3) (Daily | 19 Elm Row | Leith Walk | tel. 0131 5 56 60 66 | www.valvonacrolla.co.uk | Moderate)*; or stop by the cooler *VinCaffè* **(110 A5) (𝄞 F4)** *(Mon–Fri | 11 Multrees Walk | St Andrew Square | New Town | tel. 0131 57 00 88 | www.vincaffe.co.uk | Moderate)* for a glass of wine.

GASTRO PUBS & BISTROS

CITY CAFÉ
(114 B2) (𝄞 F5)
A true American style diner with relatively low prices for burgers and drinks. Breakfast is available from 10am to 10pm and happy hour for drinks from 5pm to 8pm. *Daily until 10pm | 19 Blair Street | Old Town | tel. 0131 2 20 01 25 | www.thecitycafe.co.uk | Budget*

KING'S WARK **(115 F2) (𝄞 L2)**
In the 17th century, this dingy, tatty building was part of King James I's building complex. Leith has now become considerably finer and this well-known, popular pub restaurant has also been spruced up. The generous servings of classic pub food (the thickest chips in town), however, remain. *Daily | 36 The Shore | Leith | tel. 0131 5 54 92 60 | www.kingswark.co.uk | buses 12, 16, 22 | Moderate*

THE DOGS **(113 F1) (𝄞 E4)**
It is a rather strange feeling to have melancholy eyes staring down at you from an XXL print while you are eating. Or to find a book with quotations about dogs (from Franz Kafka and the like) on your way to the toilet. This is supposedly due to the fact that the owner of the gastro pub only survived a depression because he had to take his dog out regularly for a walk. The menu lists hearty food from times when the Scots were not so well-off and even includes *faggots and rumbledethumps* (meat balls with baked potatoes and cabbage). *Daily | 110 Hanover Street | New Town | tel. 0131 2 20 12 08 | www.thedogsonline.co.uk | Moderate*

URBAN ANGEL ⭐ 🌐 **(113 F1) (𝄞 E4)**
The natural stone slabs on the floor signal that this shop is down to earth. The products are local; fish, game and mozzarella are Scottish, often organic and fairly traded. Lunch here is a magnet for New Townies. Tip: Take brunch at Urban Angel for the start of an angelic Sunday. *Daily | 121 Hanover Street | New Town | tel. 0131 2 25 62 15 | www.urban-angel.co.uk | Moderate*

⭐ **Valvona & Crolla**
Italian sensuality contrasts with the sober lines of the New Town → p. 53

⭐ **Urban Angel**
Edinburgh's most popular café-brasserie relies on organic products and fair trade → p. 53

⭐ **David Bann**
The best vegetarian restaurant is in the Old Town → p. 55

⭐ **The Grain Store**
Atmosphere and service are the fourth course of a splendid meal → p. 57

MARCO POLO HIGHLIGHTS

RESTAURANTS: EXPENSIVE

21212

(111 D4) (*H3*)

Permanently shining Michelin-star by Paul Kitching in a cosy and elegant townhouse on Calton Hill. You somehow feel at home, maybe because the kitchen is open plan. INSIDER TIP Wallet watching tip: 2 lunch courses from £20. *Tue–Sat | 3 Royal Terrace | New Town | tel. 0131 5 23 10 30 | www.21212restaurant.co.uk*

CASTLE TERRACE

(113 E3) (*D5*)

Chef Dominic Jack was awarded with a Michelin star just one year after opening this restaurant. The exponential success of his cooking among restaurant goers is attributed to dishes which celebrate regional ingredients and are less bombastic than those created by rival Edinburgh chefs Tom Kitchin or Mark Greenaway. Down-to-earth dishes such as plaice fillet with Ayrshire cheese are a fine tribute to Scotland's nature and a pleasure to eat. *Tue–Sat | 33/35 Castle Terrace | Old Town | tel. 0131 2 29 12 22 | www.castleterracerestaurant.com*

RESTAURANT MARK GREENAWAY

(113 E1) (*D4*)

In 2013, chef Mark Greenaway transformed a Georgian-style bank building into a Victorian stage. Mark is a star in the kitchen; his furious cooking style does not shy away from molecular gastronomy and foam, and his cuisine is to be savoured. Wine is stored in the bank's former vault. *Tue–Sat | 69 North Castle Street | New Town | tel. 0131 2 26 11 55 | www.markgreenaway.com*

FAVOURITE EATERIES

Hint of the Orient

Levantine cuisine has made a move into New Town in the shape of *Baba* (113 E1) (*D4*) *(Daily. | 130 George Street | New Town | tel. 0131 5 27 49 99 | www.baba. restaurant | Budget–Moderate)*. Mezze meals are the flavour of the month, and then there's fish and even a haggis version. Small delicacies, few calories, share and enjoy!

Off to the Caribbean

In *Trenchtown* (113 D5) (*D7*) *(Daily. | 4–8 Lochrin Buildings | Gilmore Place/ Viewforth | tel. 0131 6 23 67 86 | www. trenchtownsocial.com | Budget)* the Caribbean Social Club, the shrill decor and the island cuisine are both equally colourful. The walls are made – how original – out of oil drums and scrawled with Jamaican graffiti. Sweetcorn fritters and curried goat, bone jerk chicken with a beer in the trendy neighbourhood of Tollcross. Yummy!

The pinnacle of haute cuisine

Okay, a visit to *Restaurant Martin Wishart* (111 F2) (*L2*) *(Tue–Sat, lunch Tue–Fri | 54 The Shore | Leith | tel. 0131 5 53 35 57 | www.restaurantmartinwishart. co.uk | bus 12, 16, 22 | Expensive)* is going to cost you a pretty penny (6 course dinner from £75, lunch menu £32), but it is worth it for Scotland's top chef, with a Michelin star since 2001. The fish and meat here are regional, but the secret favourite is the 8-course vegetarian menu (£95). A glass of wine from a tenner.

Exquisite, award-winning cuisine is served in the reduced industrial atmosphere of The Kitchin

THE KITCHIN (115 E2) (*ØØ L1*)

The industrial grey tones of the interior of Tom Kitchin's extraordinary gourmet address create a feeling for the past history of this former whisky toll house. The Edinburgh chef has had his Michelin star for over ten years; he serves all that Scotland has to offer coupled with French refinement. Sea urchins, rabbit or beef – this is how straightforwardly the dishes are listed on the menu. Warning: Expensive! Reservation essential. *Tue–Sat | 78 Commercial Quay | Leith | tel. 0131 5 55 17 55 | www.thekitchin.com | buses 16, 22*

RESTAURANTS: MODERATE

DAVID BANN ★
(114 C2) (*ØØ G5*)

It is hard to imagine Scottish cooking without meat and that is what makes this excellent vegetarian restaurant in the lower Old Town so special. The risottos, *galettes*, *polentas* and homemade ravioli are delicious and can even convince meat-eaters

to sample vegetarian fare. Vegans will also find what they are looking for here. You should also try the **INSIDER TIP** *Kelpie Ale* brewed from seaweed. *Daily | 56–58 St Mary's Street | Old Town | tel. 0131 5 56 58 88 | www.davidbann.com*

HOTEL DU VIN BISTRO
(114 B3) (*ØØ F6*)

Although the hotel restaurant belongs to an exclusive chain of hotels, it has its own distinctive style. The restaurant is spacious yet intimate and modern in an atmosphere reminiscent of a castle cellar. The stylish conversion of the inner courtyard of a former mental hospital is a rare thing to find even in Edinburgh. The kitchen combines Scottish and French cuisine serving dishes such as steak and snail pie. The **INSIDER TIP** petits fours with berry marshmallows, Turkish delight or Irn-Bru, Scotland's national soft drink, are fun and delightful to taste. *Daily | 11 Bristo Place | Old Town | tel. 0131 2 47 49 00 | www.hotelduvin.com*

LOCAL SPECIALITIES

black pudding – the famous blood and oat sausage comes from Stornoway

brodick blue – ewe's milk cheese from the Island of Arran

caboc – Highland soft cheese in oatmeal

cock-a-leekie – chicken soup with leek and prunes

cranachan – full-fat whipped cream with toasted oatmeal, honey and whisky, served with raspberries

crowdie – fresh cheese from the Highlands

cullen skink – haddock soup with milk, potatoes and onions

haggis – sheep's stomach stuffed with heart, liver, lungs and oatmeal (photo left)

Irn-Bru – Scottish-made orange-coloured soft drink with caffeine, the success of which is a sore point with international companies – so far, takeover attempts have failed

kail – kale

kippers – salted, smoked herrings

oysters – those from Loch Fyne are the best

poached smoked haddock – served with poached eggs

skirlie – oatmeal groats served with onions

stovies – stewed beef with onions (leftover stew, photo right)

KALPNA

(114 C4) *(⇗ G6)*

Not just any Indian – the Gujarati/Punjabi restaurant that has been on everyone's lips for over 25 years. Naturally vegetarian and vegan. INSIDER TIP The all-you-can-eat lunch buffet. *Daily | 2–3 St Patrick Square | New Town | tel. 0131 6 67 98 90 | www.kalpnarestaurant.com*

TANG'S

(114 A3) *(⇗ F6)*

There are no frills in this Japanese restaurant. Guests are served cod in *miso* sauce on a bamboo leaf or delicious *bento* lunches, all finished off with a Japanese dessert. *Wed–Mon | 44 Candlemaker Row | Old Town | tel. 0131 2 20 50 00 | www.tangsgohan.com*

THE GRAIN STORE ★ ●
(114 A2) (*ØØ E5*)

If Michelin stars were awarded for atmosphere, as well as cool but attentive service, The Grain Store would be a candidate. Moderate prices for lunch and dinner by candlelight with bare vaulted walls: the Old Town without the kitsch. The kitchen even turns something as substantial as black pudding into a delicacy. Scottish pheasant and oysters accompanied by sinful desserts – everything is as it should be. *Daily | 20 Victoria Street | Old Town | tel. 0131 2 25 76 35 | www.grainstore-restaurant.co.uk*

Great for people watching: Olive Branch

RESTAURANTS: BUDGET

BREWHEMIA
(110 B6) (*ØØ G5*)

A bold Scottish beer hall statement that took over from a dilapidated sports bar in 2017. From delicious sexed-up porridge and sourdough flatbreads in the morning, to beer, Prosecco and burgers right up to midnight, with live bands and large tables – in short, an all-day event. Unfortunately the beer is quite expensive. *Daily | 1a Market Street | Old Town | tel. 0131 2 26 95 60 | www.brewhemia.co.uk*

OLIVE BRANCH
(110 B4) (*ØØ F3*)

This café-restaurant with its post-industrial design is one of the most popular in the fashionable Broughton district. You sit very close to your neighbours and can take in the fascinating mix of guests and also see what is going on outside on the street – thanks to the large windows. The servings of roast and fried food are extremely generous. Popular place for Sunday brunch. *Daily | 91 Broughton Street | New Town | tel. 0131 5 57 85 89 | www.theolivebranchscotland.co.uk*

LOW BUDGET

Mother India's Café (daily | 3 Infirmary Street | Old Town | tel. 0131 5 24 98 01 | www.motherindia.co.uk) serves Indian tapas for five pounds and delivers delicious takeaways to hotels.

There are some fish and chip shops that will make sure that you don't starve after midnight – large servings, often until 2am. The *Deep Sea* opposite the Playhouse Theatre on Calton Hill is one of the best.

Edinburgh has become a good address for eating inexpensively at lunchtime; you can find two-course set meals from £13. There is an especially wide choice around Grassmarket and in Broughton. The top restaurant *The Witchery & Secret Garden (daily / Castlehill | Old Town | tel. 0131 2 25 56 13 | www.thewitchery.com)* offers two-course pre- or post-theatre meals for £23.

SHOPPING

CITY WHERE TO START?
You should first head for the true Scottish shopping experience on the first quarter of the **Royal Mile (114–115 A–D 2–1)** (*E–H 4–5*). You will find real Scottish couture if you turn right onto **Victoria Street** where Armstrong's second-hand shop lies waiting between the two independent Totty Rocks and Fabhatrix boutiques. Music can be found on **Candlemaker Row. Multrees Walk** (*www.the-walk.co.uk*) is full of international haute couture. Don't miss good old **Jenners** on **Princes Street!**

Tartan kitsch is joined by top labels, especially in the New Town. The St James Centre is currently undergoing a 1 billion pound facelift.

Princes Street is the place to go if you are looking for department stores and book and electronics shops. Things are more exquisite on the parallel *George Street* and reach their peak on chic *St Andrew Square* and *Multrees Walk*. *The Royal Mile* is in the grip of tartans, oatmeal biscuits and whisky, but *Grassmarket (www.great ergrassmarket.co.uk)* and the neighbouring streets are full of charming boutiques selling fashions and accessories made in Scotland. You should not miss out on the more individual and off-beat designer shops in the gay district around *Broughton Street* or the wide range of shops in the

Design made in Scotland, chic fashions, imaginative second-hand shops and music – start your spree here!

well-off Bruntsfield area 20 minutes on foot from Princes Street. Most shops are open from 9am to 6pm from Monday to Saturday, often until 8pm on Thursday, and from 11am to 5pm on Sunday.

ART & PHOTOGRAPHY

Several New Town galleries in southern Dundas Street (109 F3–5) (*ØJ E3–4*) offer art for sale, for example traditional painting at *Anthony Woodd (4 Dundas Street)*, and contemporary art at *Fine Art*

Society (6 Dundas Street) and *The Open Eye Gallery (Ecke Abercrombie/Dundas)*. Near Waverley Station (114 B2) (*ØJ F5*) in the Old Town the *Fruitmarket Gallery (45 Market Street)* offers contemporary art and the *Stills Gallery (23 Cockburn Street)* art by Scottish photographers.

BOOKS & MUSIC

WATERSTONE'S
There is a special Edinburgh section in each of the bookshop chain's branches. They

DELICATESSEN

Cheese, cheese and more cheese: not only gourmets will sing the praises of I. J. Mellis

also offer a fine opportunity for those interested in literature to stock up on the works of Rankin, Welsh and Burns. A typical service: handwritten reviews by the staff. Open until 7pm on Sunday. *Branches: 128 Princes Street | New Town* (113 E2) *(𝄢 D5); 98/99 Ocean Terminal | Leith* (115 E1) *(𝄢 K1); www.waterstones.com*

DELICATESSEN

CROMBIES (110 B4) (𝄢 F3)
An exquisite butcher's with boar and pork "designer sausages" refined with mango, port and blue cheese. This is also the place to buy haggis for your picnic. *97–101 Broughton Street | New Town*

I. J. MELLIS (114 A2) (𝄢 E5)
Mellis has catered to the residents of the capital since 1993 and now has three fine cheese shops. Visitors will discover what the Scots are capable of making out of milk: excellent bries, cheddars and blue cheeses. You can taste *Clava Brie, Caboc,* *Connage Crowdie, Isle of Mull Cheddar* and the strong *Lanark Blue*. There is also an exquisite selection of Continental cheeses. Stock up on INSIDER TIP cheese for your picnic in Princes Street Gardens or for your stroll along the *Water of Leith. 30a Victoria Street | Old Town*

DEPARTMENT STORES

HARVEY NICHOLS ★ (114 A1) (𝄢 F4)
The building of the most exclusive British department store on aristocratic St Andrew Square is unassuming compared with the luxurious goods hanging from the pegs and on the shelves inside. Shirts from Alexander McQueen, suits made by the most famous Saville Row tailor, Gieves & Hawkes, as well as the usual international brands. There is a restaurant with a view of the square on the upper floor. The selection of whiskies in front of it will make connoisseurs go weak at the knees: A bottle of whisky, even of Japanese provenance, can command a four-

figure price tag. Recover from the shock with sushi or in the Chocolate Lounge. *30–34 St Andrew Square | New Town | www.harveynichols.com*

JENNERS ●
(114 A1) *(ᗰ F4)*

Jenners' Victorian façade is especially striking; it has occupied the corner of Princes Street since 1838. Jenners is a confusing labyrinth of around 100 departments and is unique in the world of renowned department stores partly because of this. But that is exactly why you should pop in and admire the high-ceilinged grand hall before getting lost. You will meet half of Edinburgh during your expedition and they will probably look just as confused as you. The lifts travel at a snail's pace, the escalators are well-hidden; in a word, Jenners is the perfect place to get out of the rain. You can buy almost anything there although the emphasis is on clothing and material. A Chinese investor took over the quintessential Edinburgh department store in 2014, but left its distinguished name intact. *48 Princes Street | New Town*

FASHION

21ST CENTURY KILTS ★
(113 F1) *(ᗰ E4)*

Men who wear kilts pose a genuine threat to female fashion domination. The kilts made by Howie Nicholsby give men plenty of room to stretch their legs and appear traditional and avant-garde at the same time. They can be worn with Crocs, shoes or parachutist's boots. Shoes with low heels make these kilts of wool, leather or even PVC real eye-catchers – that's presumably what metrosexuality is all about. *48 Thistle Street | New Town | www.21stcenturykilts.com*

ANTA (114 A3) *(ᗰ E5)*

Tartan without the kitsch! Annie Stewart uses the gentle colours of Scotland's Highlands and coasts in her exquisite woollen blankets, carpets, handbags, suitcases and even porcelain. You won't

---

MARCO POLO HIGHLIGHTS

FASHION

find any better in Edinburgh. *119 George Street | New Town | www.anta.co.uk*

ARMSTRONG & SON ★
(114 A3) (*ᗰ E5*)
Second-hand since 1840! Armstrong sold vintage clothes here before vintage was en vogue. Kylie Minogue and Franz Ferdinand have found something here from the good old times. Of course, there is not only Brit-retro from the past centuries but also kilts (from £20), not to forget the *sporran* – the pouch worn with a kilt (from £40). *83 Grassmarket | Old Town | www.armstrongsvintage.co.uk*

BILL BABER (114 A3) (*ᗰ E5*)
The knitwear designer describes the personal style of his unique label as a cross between handcraft and fashion. Linen in particular, but also merino, cotton and silk are used in the production of pullovers, capes and jackets that all takes place in a back room.*66 Grassmarket | Old Town | www.billbaber.com*

THE BROTIQUE (113 E1) (*ᗰ E4*)
Men! Round off your hipster outfit here with choice accessories. Even if it's just the tweed cover for your iPad. *39 Queen Street | New Town | www.thebrotique.co.uk*

CORNICHE (114 B2) (*ᗰ G5*)
Unpretentious boutique with intriguing if expensive individual items – although sometimes good bargains can be had, too. Worth a visit just to see Vivienne Westwood's, Ivan Grundahl's and Novemb3r's creations. In addition, playful "kilt-like" trousers for men. *2 Jeffrey Street | Old Town | www.corniche.org.uk*

INSIDER TIP ▶ FABHATRIX
(114 A3) (*ᗰ F5*)
Sherlock Holmes' deerstalker hats made of Harris Tweed for the men, wispy fascina-

tors for the women, and every conceivable kind of felt, woollen or silk, hand-made headwear. Fawns Reid is the most sought-after milliner in Edinburgh. *13 Cowgatehead | Old Town | www.fabhatrix.com*

GEORGE STREET ★
(113 E–F1) (*ᗰ D–E4*)
The most aristocratic axis through the New Town is the place to look for classic fashion – unflustered and pleasantly understated. It invites visitors to take a stroll past the clothes shops. You will find respected outfitters including yuppie Brits like Jack Wills, the American Brooks Brothers, Church's, the time-honoured shoemakers, Laura Ashley, Karen Millen and Jigsaw for ladies, Moss for the man in his elegant suit, as well as the classic shirt-maker T. M. Lewin. Many shops are open until 5pm on Sunday. *New Town | www.edinburghgeorge street.co.uk*

JOEY D ★
(110 A–B4) (*ᗰ F3*)
Unique items for men and women made of recycled material. The designer Joey D even made Elton John chic! The most outlandish appliqués and vivid prints, but always wearable. Clothes are first cut up and then reassembled to form new creations. The handbags are the most unconventional articles. Creative, urban, sexy – and, of course with a bit of tartan. *54 Broughton Street | New Town*

MULTREES WALK
(114 A1) (*ᗰ F4*)
This small street on the eastern side of St Andrews Square in the New Town has developed into the right place to buy top international brands such as Armani, Louis Vuitton, Mulberry and the like. *St Andrew Square | New Town | www. the-walk.co.uk*

TOTTY ROCKS
(114 A2) *(🚇 E5)*

The wonderful designers and fashion teachers Holly Blackburn and Lynsey Michell are among the top acts in the young Scottish fashion industry. In the meantime they even dress the premier Nicola Sturgeon. Their INSIDER TIP melancholic-fun mac-chic fashion label has now attracted celebrity clients. *45–47 Barclay Terrace | New Town | www.tottyrocks.co.uk*

JEWELLERY

SHEILA FLEET JEWELLERY ★
(109 D4) *(🚇 D3)*

The jewellery designer has let the magical flair of her home on the Orkney Islands flow into her creations. For example, in her "Rowan Collection" Sheila Fleet adapts details of the Scottish landscape and the reflection of the moon on the sea to create a delicate interpretation of the Highland rowan in jewellery. The changing tide, pebbles rounded by the sea and the colours at the edge of pools of water at low tide can be felt in her pieces and make it difficult to resist buying them. *18 St Stephen Street | Stockbridge*

MARKETS & WINDOW SHOPPING

BRUNTSFIELD PLACE
(113 D–E6) *(🚇 D8)*

Would you like to spend a couple of hours in a nearby suburb with charming cafés, bakeries and souvenir shops without any of the usual Scottish kitsch? Bruntsfield is only a twenty-minute walk from the Royal Mile and is also easy to reach by bus. There are boutiques selling wooden toys, jewellery, novel wallpaper, shoes and children's clothing – the selection is first-rate. *Buses 11, 16, 23, 27*

Pioneer in retro clothing, still with a cult character: Armstrong & Son

FARMER'S MARKET ● (113 E3) (*[map] D5*)
The weekly speciality market at the castle is the first place you should visit on Saturday. There is nothing else like it in Edinburgh and you will get a good overview of all the fish, cheese, pickles and vegetables that can be bought there. If you have not had breakfast, you can even start the day here with take-away porridge. *Sat 9am–2pm | Castle Terrace | Old Town*

INSIDER TIP ▶ RAEBURN PLACE
(108–109 C–D3) (*[map] B–C3*)
There is row of shops next to each other along the main street in Stockbridge (to the west of the Water of Leith). This is where the locals buy their fish, second-hand books, tea and go to the hairdresser. The street will almost make you feel you are in a village; there is a lot to see in the shops and pubs and you will find some

real bargains – how about Dickens' *Oliver Twist* complete with a bookmark for next to nothing. *Stockbridge*

MUSIC

Glasgow is more up to date in terms of music. But some of the record shops here seem to have been biding their time for the vinyl revival. *Record Shak* (114 C5) (*[map] G7*) *(69 Clerk Street), Hogs Head Music* (114 C5) (*[map] G7*) *(62 South Clerk Street)* and *Ripping Records* (114 B2) (*[map] F5*) *(92 South Bridge)* are treasure troves. *Underground Solu'shn* (114 A2) (*[map] F5*) *(9 Cockburn Street)* attracts DJs, *Fopp* (114 A1) (*[map] E4*) *(3–15 Rose Street)* has the biggest selection. Music shops are the best places to find **INSIDER TIP ▶** info and tickets for live acts.

TRADITIONAL SCOTTISH

CONCRETE WARDROBE
(110 B4) (*[map] F3*)
A wonderful gallery belonging to a textile designer, where you're sure to find a Scottish touch for the table, wall or sofa at home among a selection of pieces by a variety of artisans. *50a Broughton Street | New Town | www.concretewardrobe.com*

HAWICK CASHMERE
(114 A3) (*[map] E5*)
The lightweight, expensive goats' wool comes from China and Mongolia but it has been processed in the small town of Hawick in the south of Scotland since 1874. Luxury knitwear brand whose traditional goods are famous worldwide. *71–81 Grassmarket | Old Town | www.hawico.com/en*

KINLOCH ANDERSON (115 E2) (*[map] L1*)
An institution: Highland dress at its best has been sold here since 1868. This is a serious kilt shop for connoisseurs and

---

LOW BUDGET

Whoever is looking for eccentric accessories, unusual souvenirs or Scottish indie designer goods, the old-town boutique *Hannah Zakari (43 Candlemaker Row | www.hannahzakari.co.uk)* specialises in handmade high-quality items sold at affordable prices. Their diverse collection of items ranges from indie necklaces to smartphone covers made of Tweed as well as art prints, notebooks, brooches etc.

There are frequent sales with slashed prices – you might find a £800 Dolce & Gabbana lady's jacket for as little as £50 at *Harvey Nichols* on *St Andrew Square.* Or simply look around *Multrees Walk.*

those who want to become one. Take the plunge. *4 Dock Street | Leith*

ROYAL MILE WHISKIES ⭐
(114 A2) (*𝄞 F5*)

It is said that the shop has more than 300 kinds of whisky in stock and you are

SCOTTISH WHISKY HERITAGE CENTRE
(113 F2) (*𝄞 E5*)

A tour through the history of whisky will put you in the right mood to buy a bottle or two of the almost 280 kinds on sale here. The shop near the castle also sees whisky as a form of entertainment.

Don't even try to count them: there are more than 300 kinds of whisky at Royal Mile Whiskies

welcome to taste them. However, it makes more sense to be completely sober and let the imaginative labels and names inspire you when you make your choice. *379 High Street | Old Town*

SCOTTISH DESIGNER KNITWEAR
(114 A3) (*𝄞 F5–6*)

This canyon of a street in the Old Town might appear rather gloomy but the colours and vivacity of the fashions designed by Joyce Forsyth will make you forget it. Knitwear to clothe the lady with a taste for unusual patterns from head to toe. *42 Candlemaker Row | Old Town | www. joyceforsyth.co.uk*

354 Castlehill | Old Town | www.scotch whiskyexperience.co.uk

WHISKY SHOP
(114 A2) (*𝄞 E5*)

The finest whisky shop in Edinburgh steeped in atmosphere. An estimated 500 labels are stacked up in this relatively small shop, including its own brand: *Glenkeir Treasures*. Customers can do a whisky tasting between the casks and bottles. The **INSIDER TIP** 200 and 500 ml bottles of whisky filled directly from the cask are sure to delight whisky lovers. *28 Victoria Street | Old Town | www. whiskyshop.com*

ENTERTAINMENT

CITY WHERE TO START?
A cocktail in the exuberant and beery Old Town, e.g. at the **Dragonfly (113 F3)** (*⫯ E6*) is a good place to start for everyone. The debauched nightlife is just a few yards away, between **Grassmarket** and **Cowgate**. Fans of the more fashionable New Town style navigate towards the area between **St Andrew** and **George Square**. **Broughton** has a lively gay scene in the *pink triangle*. Lovers of good jazz will head for the Jazz Bar before moving on to the Royal Oak for a midnight folk jam session.

Edinburgh also shows what it is capable of at night. The action starts in the small clubs, cinemas or in one of the countless pubs. The atmosphere in Edinburgh is more lounge-like than loud, more folk and jazz than rock.

The evening usually gets underway in a pub either in one of the many cocktail bars in the New Town or with a pint in the pub. This is usually accompanied by top-fermented ale rather than a glass of wine. If this is what you are looking for, the area between Raeburn Place and Circus Place in *Stockbridge* will meet your requirements. At the busy *Tollcross* corner the ladies' skirts are shorter and their heels higher but this is also where you will find the best theatre. *George Street* has the reputation of being posh and this makes

Edinburgh's nightlife isn't wild as such. But it's quirky and the old vaulted cellars are often crowded and full of music

the queues in front of the clubs longer. The pub scene around *Grassmarket* in the Old Town promises a lively start. ★ *Leith* has developed into a popular place to go out and have fun in the evening.

BARS, PUBS & CAFÉS

BAILIE BAR (109 D4) *(ᗰ D3)*
The bar counter turns a full 360 degrees and there are probably at least the same number of drinks served here. With its cosy location in a cellar, the pub attracts

students, bankers and sport-TV fans. In keeping with the trendy area near the bridge over the Leith, it serves good bar food *(Budget)*. *Daily 11am–midnight | 2–4 St Stephen Street | Stockbridge*

BENNET'S BAR (113 E5) *(ᗰ D7)*
Wonderful Victorian décor including separées for women that were fashionable at the time; all of this with plenty of brass, wood and large colourful windows (this also makes it a good place to visit during the day). It is next to the *King's*

Theatre and this means that the long bar is packed after performances. Theatre audiences apparently also like live rugby. Clearly more locals than tourists. *Sun–Wed 11am–11:30pm, Thu–Sat 11am–1pm | 8 Leven Street | Old Town*

Brauhaus is a paradise for beer fans

BRAUHAUS (113 E4) (𝄚 D6)

A popular small beer bar. You should make sure that you still have your wits about you when you go in so that you can make the right selection from the 360 different kinds of beer served. As the night progresses, the friendly barman will take care of that for you. Don't forget to have something to eat while you are trying the brew – maybe a pretzel? Young crowd, students and civilised football fans (TV). *Daily noon–1am | 105–107 Lauriston Place | Old Town*

CAFÉ ROYAL CIRCLE BAR ★
(114 A1) (𝄚 F4)

This is probably the most magnificent bar in town with its listed Victorian furnishings. The bar forms an island in between walls decorated with tile paintings from 1886 showing prominent inventors – Benjamin Franklin, Isaac Newton, Michael Faraday, James Watt, etc. – looking down on the crowd of locals and tourists. Try the Shetland mussels from the kitchen of the attached Oyster Bar. The *Guildford Arms* at *no. 1–5* on the same street is rather similar. *Mon–Wed 11am–11pm, Thu until midnight, Fri, Sat until 1am, Sun 12:30–11pm | 19 West Register Street | New Town*

CALEY SAMPLE ROOMS
(112 A6) (𝄚 A8)

Great gastro pub serving home-grown food and some 🟢 dishes. Recommendation: smoked fish cakes! It offers a superb range of ales and co. reflecting Edinburgh's new-found love of beer. INSIDER TIP Organises special tasting events together with chefs and microbreweries. *Daily until midnight or 1am | 42–58 Angle Park Terrace | West | buses 1, 4, 34, 44*

INSIDER TIP HALFWAY HOUSE
(114 B2) (𝄚 F5)

The Halfway House is a hidden meeting place for the locals. The smallest pub in Edinburgh is located on the landing of one of the typical steep streets between the Royal Mile and Waverley Station. But there is still enough room for four ale taps at the bar and 30 different malts behind it. The meals that come out of the tiny kitchen are solid hits: pheasant soup, wild boar sausages with mashed potatoes or typical Scottish *cullen skink* (smoked fish soup) are all freshly prepared using ingredients from Scottish companies *(Budget)*. *Daily from 11am | 24 Fleshmarket Close | Old Town*

HANGING BAT (113 E3) (*Ⓜ D6*)
More of a brewery with stools than a pub. Besides an exhaustive range of 150 beers, there are also a few gins and wines. INSIDER**TIP** Draught beer is not offered in pints but in smaller glasses for more freshness and enjoyment. Hotdogs and burgers are served as an accompaniment. *Daily from noon | 133 Lothian Road | Old Town*

HECTORS (109 D3–4) (*Ⓜ C3*)
Popular bar with candlelight, cosy corners and the latest music – with DJs at the weekend – that draws in Edinburgh's well-heeled, middle-class crowd. Fantastic Saturday brunch, pub quiz on Sundays. *Daily 9am–1am | 47–49 Deanhaugh Street | Stockbridge*

JUNIPER (110 A5) (*Ⓜ F4*)
A classier source of Prosecco or cocktails in the early evening, instead of subterranean creepiness, when the view from the window sweeps over Princes Street to the Old Town. *Daily from noon | 20 Princes Street | New Town*

INSIDER**TIP** **SHEEP HEID INN**
(117 D2) (*Ⓜ L7*)
The oldest pub in Scotland (1360) has welcomed countless guests and is now famous for its tasty food (Sunday lunch!). From parliament it's a pleasurable walk (1 hour) around Arthur's Seat, no matter which direction. The village of Duddingston, the loch, the pub and Dr Neil's Garden: all very relaxing (see also Discovery Tour p. 93). *Daily until 11pm | 43–45 The Causeway | Duddingston | bus 4, 44, 113*

TEUCHTERS LANDING
(115 E–F 1–2) (*Ⓜ L1*)
A balmy summer evening and nowhere to go? Catch a bus to Leith and grab a

table at the popular beer garden at the shore behind the cosy, up-scale pub restaurant *A Room in Leith (Budget–Moderate)*. The building is a bit difficult to find; it is one of the remnants of the former customs and ferry port. *Daily 10:30am–midnight | 1c Dock Place | Leith | bus 12, 16, 22, 23, 300*

INSIDER**TIP** **THE BANSHEE LABYRINTH**
(114 B2) (*Ⓜ F5*)
The labyrinthine subterranean Banshee has three bar areas, seven crypt-like rooms, jukeboxes, a dance floor complete with pole and a small non-stop cinema,

---

MARCO POLO HIGHLIGHTS

★ **Leith**
The old port has become the most popular place to go out → p. 67

★ **Café Royal Circle Bar**
Perfect beer and extravagant Victorian pub elegance → p. 68

★ **The Voodoo Rooms**
Magnificently flamboyant event and cocktail bar → p. 71

★ **Cabaret Voltaire**
First-rate music cellar with dance club; the best of its kind → p. 71

★ **Sandy Bell's**
Daily folk-music sessions with local and international stars → p. 72

★ **Festival Theatre**
Edinburgh's top theatre for plays, opera and dance → p. 72

The Voodoo Rooms are a great location to while the night away in Edinburgh

poetry slams and zombie parties. Excellent DJ mix or live gigs: there are even cosy corners for a "candlelight burger". The "shocking" action starts around 10pm, as do the karaoke sessions, Sun, Tue and Wed. *Daily | 29–35 Niddry Street | Old Town*

THE DOME
(110 A5) *(ഈ E4)*

This ex-bank looks like a temple with its pompous façade on George Street and a rear entrance with a garden terrace onto bustling Rose Street. Posh locals meet here under the chandeliers hanging from the 50 ft-high ceilings for their *latte*, lunch or dinner. Confidently *chic*. *Daily | 14 George Street | New Town*

THE STOCKBRIDGE TAP
(109 D3–4) *(ഈ C3)*

With its light wood, parquet floors without carpets and cheerful neighbourhood atmosphere, this pub in the centre of Stockbridge is absolutely un-Victorian. Six draft ales, any number of different kinds of whisky and a small menu with substantial British food, including a delicious pheasant casserole *(Budget)*. *Tue–Sun from noon | 2 Raeburn Place | Stockbridge*

CLUBS

DRAGONFLY
(113 F3) *(ഈ E6)*

The ageing top dog among the old-school cocktail bars. In keeping with the Old Town, the feeling is more pub with nightclub than stylish bar. Still: cult status and phenomenal cocktails. *52 West Port | Old Town | www.dragonflycocktailbar.com*

OPAL LOUNGE
(113 F1) *(ഈ E4)*

Chic-quirky George Street scene. The furnishings as well as the clothes of the late-

CINEMAS

Although the people of Edinburgh like going to the cinema and the city would provide a great setting for films, comparatively few are made here. Most of the cult film *Trainspotting* was actually shot in Glasgow. The program schedule changes on Fridays. You can find out what's showing in the daily newspapers.

CAMEO PICTUREHOUSE ●
(113 E4) *(ᛗ D7)*
This listed art house cinema is one of Scotland's oldest film houses still in use and is a venue for the *Edinburgh International Film Festival.* Cinema 1 is the most charming of its three auditoriums. Comfortable setting with elegant seating and ample legroom. Inviting bar – drinks can be taken into the auditorium. *Admission from 8 £| 38 Home Street | Old Town*

FILMHOUSE (113 E3) *(ᛗ D6)*
The *Edinburgh Film Festival* is held in mid-June in the most interesting cinema, from the artistic point of view, in the city. The Filmhouse concentrates on classic films and relatively unknown features, as well as subtitled foreign-language films. *Admission from £8 | 88 Lothian Road | Old Town | www.filmhousecinema.com*

night clubbers are very stylish. Good dance scene. You should take a partner with you; it is difficult to make contact here. It is especially popular and trendy after 10pm – the queues waiting to get in show that. Soul and hip-hop. *Sun–Fri 5pm–3am, Sat noon–3am, food until 10pm | admission after 10pm from £6 | 51a George Street | New Town | www.opallounge.co.uk*

THE VOODOO ROOMS ★
(114 A1) *(ᛗ F4)*
In bombastic Victorian design, the trendiest lounge, cocktail and event bar is located above the more exclusive Café Royal and Oyster Bar. This is the place to be seen, offering cocktails, live-music bands and cabaret performances. Elegant chillout salon with subtle lighting, ballroom and "opium den" setting. Unpretentious pre-theatre dinner. *Sun–Thu 2pm–1am, Fri, Sat noon–3am | admission from £6 | 19a West Register Street | www.thevoodoorooms.com*

LIVE MUSIC

CABARET VOLTAIRE ★
(114 B2) *(ᛗ F5)*
Most popular venue for live gigs and album presentations in the subterranean heart of the Old Town. The club, with its multiple stages and dancefloors, only closes at 3am. Weekend tip: Japanese street food. Interesting from 7pm onwards. *Admission free or up to £20 | 36 Blair Street | Old Town | www.thecabaret voltaire.com*

THE JAZZ BAR (114 B3) *(∅ F5)*

Up to five gigs take place every evening in the groovy cellar with its small stage. It becomes funkier after 9pm at weekends when a DJ takes over. A small admission fee is charged for each performance. ● *Teatime Acoustic Tue–Sun 6pm– 8:30pm, Early Gig daily 8:30–11:30pm, Late Night Slot 11:30pm–3am | 1a Chambers Street | Old Town | www.thejazz bar.co.uk*

INSIDER TIP ROYAL OAK (114 B3) *(∅ G5)*

During the day, this is about as empty as a pub can be. But later in the evening, the two small bars on the ground floor and in the basement fill up and the air vibrates with the sound of strings, bows and – usually smoky – voices. Folk music so exciting it will even make your beer froth. *Daily 9am–2am | 1 Infirmary Street | Old Town*

LOW BUDGET

A night with drinks, good DJs and live acts doesn't cost the world in *The Bongo Club (66 Cowgate | Old Town)*. Young Edinburghers love it.

A summer evening in the *Cumberland Bar (1–3 Cumberland Street)* is so attractive because, even with the good pub food and the fresh air in the beer garden, the night will not be too expensive.

Leith is upmarket with its Michelin stars. The more affordable counterpart is the postindustrial street-food market hall *The Pitt (125 Pitt Street)*. For more budget food: *www.eh1. com/category/foodie/budget-eats*

SANDY BELL'S ★ ● (114 A3) *(∅ F6)*

Typical, simple pub that does not serve food near Greyfriars Cemetery. However, it really comes alive in the afternoon and evening when local and international folk-music stars get together for a jam session. Fiddles, guitars, singing: Celtic lifestyle at its best. *Daily 11am–1am | 25 Forrest Road | Old Town*

GAY & LESBIAN

Edinburgh's *pink triangle* is located in the New Town between Broughton Street and the Leith Walk end of Princes Street (112 B–C 2–3) *(∅ F–G 2–3)*. Not only the gay and lesbian crowd dines and parties here. The *CC Blooms (daily 11am–3am | 23 Greenside Place)* is both a restaurant and party location. Next door, *Café Habana (daily 1pm–1am | 22 Greenside Place)* invites you in for a drink; *Chalky's (daily 4pm– 1am | 4 Picardy Place)* is a hot dance spot; *Regent Bar (daily 11am–1am | Montrose Terrace)* is a sophisticated gay pub.

The scene is booming, endorsed by the legislation of the Scottish Parliament to legalise same-sex marriage several years ago. Further information available at: *black-kilt-tours.org/edinburgh-gay-bars*

THEATRE & CLASSICAL MUSIC

FESTIVAL THEATRE ★

(114 B3) *(∅ G6)*

This is the most prestigious theatre in Edinburgh, not only during the Festival. Modern dance, opera, drama – all the top names perform here. Stylish mixture of an old theatre building and modern glass architecture. The art nouveau/Beaux Arts temple of the muses, with its impressive decor, can seat a good 1900 guests. The café is more modern; delicious lunch. *£8–60 | 13–29 Nicolson Street | Old Town | www.edtheatres.com/festival*

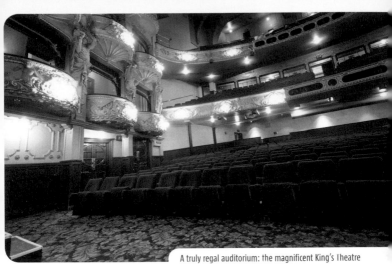

A truly regal auditorium: the magnificent King's Theatre

KING'S THEATRE (113 E5) (*D7*)

A theatre out of an old picture book: wood, marble and gold leaf create an elegant setting for plays, musicals, comedies and opera. There are pubs next door so you can knock back a quick pint during the interval. This is where Sean Connery made his first appearance as an actor. *From £12 | 2 Leven Street | Old Town | www.edtheatres.com/kings*

PLAYHOUSE (110 B4) (*G3*)

International stars from Steely Dan and Tom Waits to Katie Melua, as well as musical shows appear in this large auditorium with 3,000 seats on Calton Hill. Also a venue for well-known British stand-up comedians. *From £12 | 18–22 Greenside Place | New Town | www.playhousetheatre.com*

ROYAL LYCEUM THEATRE
(113 E3) (*D6*)

The classics and occasionally contemporary plays are performed in a beautiful Victorian building from 1883. It is even said that a ghost haunts the gallery. As many as eight plays are staged annually, making the Royal Lyceum, in its own words, the largest dramatic theatre in Scotland. *From £15 | Grindlay Street | Old Town | www.lyceum.org.uk*

TRAVERSE THEATRE (113 E3) (*D5*)

The centre of contemporary Scottish theatre. Fans of these types of performances will find what they are looking for on the stage in the cellar; those who want to sample Edinburgh's theatrical air should visit the INSIDER TIP ▶ *Traverse Bar Café*. Popular Festival Fringe meeting point. *Free or up to £25 | 10 Cambridge Street | Old Town | www.traverse.co.uk*

USHER HALL (113 E2) (*D5*)

This circular theatre is the venue for the most important concerts of classical music during the Edinburgh Festival. At other times, there are concerts with symphony orchestras, jazz stars and rock bands. The main organ is a real treasure. *From £18 | Castle Steps/Lothian Road | Old Town | www.usherhall.co.uk*

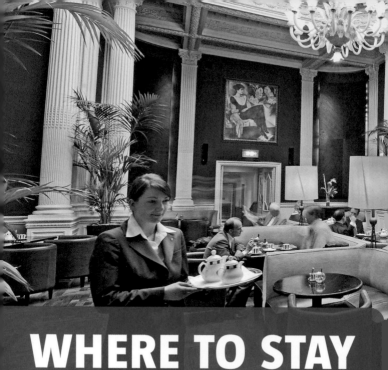

WHERE TO STAY

In spite of its relatively small size, Edinburgh has a wide variety of hotels with a total of 23,000 beds, many of them in small guesthouses. But even that number is hardly enough during the Festival weeks in summer and at Hogmanay (31 December). Then everything is hopelessly booked out.

There is a good selection of charming, traditional grand hotels and trendy boutique hotels in the luxury segment. They might be a bit more than your average holiday budget but most of them also have a brasserie, café or nightclub on the premises that make it possible for people not staying there to take a look inside. Another alternative are the bed-and-breakfast lodgings that are often a little out of town. Breakfast is, of course, included in the price, otherwise you will pay around £7 for a continental breakfast or £13 for the Scottish variety. Two or three-star hotel chains have little individual character and will probably even make you forget what a magnificent city you are in while you are there overnight. That makes staying in one of the Georgian townhouses from the 18th and 19th centuries even more recommendable, where you stay in typically high-ceilinged rooms and can enjoy personal hospitality – along with sometimes draughty sash windows and thick quilts on the bed. The widely varying prices of double rooms in these hotels in the former homes of the wealthier classess (£80–180), however, do usually include breakfast. A sign with stars issued by the Scottish Tourism Society at the

There is a huge choice of boutique hotels, townhouses and guesthouses – but Edinburgh is bursting at the seams during the Festival

door of a hotel is a useful aid in determining its quality. The prices of rooms can easily double during the Festival, over public holidays and when international rugby games are scheduled – especially in August and December. There is usually a considerable reduction in prices otherwise between October and March. If you look at the websites of the boutique hotels, you will often find amazing special offers! The number of apartments and Airbnbs on offer has doubled in just two years *(www.edlets.com)*.

HOTELS: EXPENSIVE

CHESTER RESIDENCE ●
(112 C2) (𝓂 B5)

Large apartments in Edwardian terrace houses in the peaceful West End. High ceilings, kitchen, cool design and sound system, luxuriously furnished in muted colours. The reception is staffed around the clock, arranges breakfast and can help out with almost any wish. INSIDER TIP Guests feel like they are staying in an upper-class home with discrete personnel. *23 apartments |*

9 Rothesay Place | New Town | tel. 0131 2 26 20 75 | www.chester-residence.com

HOTEL DU VIN ★
(114 A–B3) (*M* F6)

This hidden house is a medium-sized, luxury boutique hotel that successfully blends the charm of a building in with the requirements of a modern hotel such as the discreet insertion of double glazing into the original two-part sash windows. The rooms are luxurious but practical, the

Nira Caledonia: a reflection of luxury

delightful details elegant, the service exceptional. There is an exquisitely-stocked wine bar and a room for whisky tasting. The bistro restaurant has the intimate atmosphere of a wine store; the inner courtyard provides a modern contrast to the surrounding Old Town. *47 rooms | 11 Bristo Place | Old Town | tel. 0131 2 85 14 79 | www.hotelduvin.com*

MALMAISON (113 F1) (*M* L1)

This building, which looks like a city *palais*, at the port in Leith is one of the first boutique hotels. It was built in 1833 as a home for sailors and is now the flagship hotel of the Scottish Malmaison company – a somewhat old-fashioned *grandseigneur* of the hotel business. Here and there, the luxury is a bit frayed, but the grand-hotel atmosphere has been preserved. The guests live directly on the water not far from the new lifestyle scenery in the old port. Restaurant and bar. *100 rooms | 1 Tower Place | Leith | tel. 0131 4 69 50 00 | www.malmaison.com*

LE MONDE (113 F1) (*M* E4)

This luxurious boutique hotel on the exclusive shopping street has received several awards. The rooms are each dedicated to the style of an individual world city. Flamboyant restaurant with slightly less flamboyant food. An in-house nightclub that also attracts students during the week. *18 rooms | 16 George Street | New Town | tel. 0131 2 70 39 00 | www.lemondehotel.co.uk*

NIRA CALEDONIA ★ (109 D4) (*M* D3)

Cool New Town elegance and great service are at the top of the agenda in this Georgian townhouse. The handful of rooms vary greatly due to a preservation order, from between 13 and 42 m². Boutique, but unique, with a hipster touch in the hipster city village of Stockbridge. A successful balancing act between old and new Edinburgh extravagance. Great food. *28 rooms | 6–10 Gloucester Place | Stockbridge | tel. 0131 2 25 27 20 | www.niracaledonia.com*

THE RUTLAND HOTEL ★
(113 D2) (*M* D5)

The Scottish "Style Awards" named this small luxury boutique hotel best in its class

The master of house, Calvin Harris, is waiting above your bed in Angel's Share Hotel

immediately after it was opened. The location in the West End opens up views of the neighbouring castle and Calton Hill. The rooms are individually designed, not over-decorated. By the way, this is where the father of antiseptic surgery, Joseph Lister (1827–1912), once lived – one of the great minds working in this city. The hotel's restaurant *Kyloe Restaurant & Grill (www.kyloerestaurant.com | Moderate)* – is an excellent addition to the hotel. In spacious and spectacular design, the steakhouse boasts enviable views from its large windows – the splendid ground-floor bar *The Huxley (www.thehuxley.co.uk)* is also inviting. *12 rooms | 1–3 Rutland Street | Old Town | tel. 0131 2 29 34 02 | www.therutlandhotel.com*

HOTELS: MODERATE

ANGEL'S SHARE HOTEL
(113 D2) (*∅ D5*)
The former post office between Charlotte Square and the west end of Princes Street now has the charm of a well-designed city hotel. Huge framed portraits of famous Scots – for example Robert Carlyle from "Trainspotting" – watch over

---

MARCO POLO HIGHLIGHTS

★ **Nira Caledonia**
Upper-class villa atmosphere with hipster elegance → p. 76

★ **Hotel du Vin**
Elegant and hip: architecturally revitalised building → p. 76

★ **The Rutland Hotel**
Style and castle views → p. 76

★ **The Inn on the Mile**
Quirky modernism with view of the Royal Mile → p. 79

★ **Grassmarket Hotel**
Great location for night owls → p. 79

your sleep. Breakfast is taken in the magnificent bar. The building is in a prime location at the juncture between Old Town, New Town and Dean Village. *31 rooms | 9–11 Hope Street | tel. 0131 2 47 70 00 | www.angelssharehotel.com*

INSIDER TIP CANDLEMAKER ROW
(114 A3) (*ω F6*)
This flat in an 18th-century house near Greyfriars Cemetery is intended for a maximum of four people. You can leave the hustle and bustle of the Old Town outside the thick walls of this modern, comfortable and well-equipped flat. It is

best to reserve for a week or for days that are free between two other bookings. It's best to book well in advance! *Weekly rate £400–500 | 48/1 Candlemaker Row | Old Town | tel. 0131 5 38 03 52 | www.edin burghselfcatering.biz*

EQ2-FOUNTAINCOURT APARTMENTS
You can live very comfortably in these apartments at eight different locations, most in the West End: kitchen, luxurious bathroom, home-entertainment system and even a parking space in the heart of town. The price is reduced according to the length of your stay. Breakfast packs for

MORE THAN A GOOD NIGHT'S SLEEP

Very, very grand
The Balmoral **(114 B1)** (*ω F4*) *(188 rooms | 1 Princes Street | tel. 0131 5 56 24 14 | short.travel/edi17 | Expensive)* exudes the feeling of grand hotel from every ostentatious pore, its Victorian clock tower (which gives you a three-minute buffer to your train departing from neighbouring Waverley Station) forcing its way into view from many locations. You can give it a moderate test run, for example with tea in the fantastic Palm Court, then take it a step further with a meal in the starred restaurant *Number One (Expensive)* and end up checking into a room or suite. It doesn't get any grander, from £180 without breakfast, in winter.

The epitome of hospitality
Anyone who spends the night at *Brunton Bothy* **(111 D4)** (*ω H3*) *(2 rooms | Brunton Place | New Town | tel. 0131 78 75 33 35 39 | www.facebook.com/brunton bothy | Moderate)* is sure to fall in love

with their hosts Dave and Tokes, and the tastefulness with which they have styled their small B&B themselves – they call, it with an ironic wink, bothy (refuge hut). You will feel like a guest of honour without being fussed over. One night is not enough! Probably the best Airbnb in the city. Located on Calton Hill.

Waterbed XXL
On the 55 ft by 10 ft houseboat *The Four Sisters Boatel Hotel* **(113 D4)** (*ω D7*) *(Lochrin Basin | tel. 0131 3 36 40 57 | www.thefoursisters.co.uk)* on Union Canal you will sleep like a log and completely against the flow. The space inside the ship, which is decked out with light-coloured wood, is large enough for four adults and two children. Self catering, breakfast on deck and four minutes from Grassmarket by folding bike. There's certainly no lack of modern furnishings and accessories. This cosy romantic experience is affordable too: £100–220 (depending on the season).

You solve sudoku puzzles in your sleep at the Grassmarket Hotel

four can be purchased as an extra. Look out for offers. *150 flats | tel. 0131 6 22 66 77 | www.fountaincourtapartments.com*

GRASSMARKET HOTEL ★
(114 A3) (*ØØ E5*)
Ideally situated not far from Edinburgh's enjoyable spots. If you are looking to stay in the relaxed Old Town surrounded by pubs and popular restaurants, the Grassmarket is in the perfect location below the city's castle. The small rooms are super functional, clean, minimalistic in design and equipped with all the mod cons such as iPod docks. *45 rooms | 94–96 Grassmarket | Old Town | tel. 0131 2 20 22 99 | www.festival-inns.co.uk*

THE INN ON THE MILE ★
(114 B2) (*ØØ F5*)
So many facets! Its central location in the Old Town, the temple-like entrance, its past as a bank and the great lively bar with live acts all suggest quirky room design. The opulent staircase with luxury wallpaper from Glasgow's Timorous Beasties is far from subtle either. The rooms are, however, so bright and serenely modern that you can really relax away from the hustle and bustle here. Tip: 10 percent off spa treatments at INSIDER TIP *Zen Lifestyle (Teviot Place)* (10 min) *9 rooms | 82 High Street | Old Town | tel. 0131 5 56 99 40 | theinnonthemile.co.uk*

THE RAEBURN
(108 C3) (*ØØ C2*)
As if you were wrapping yourself up in Scotland's dark saturated colours and tartan textiles. The ten rooms are individual with elegant accessories. The restaurant and pub make it a meeting place for the slightly dandyish Stockbridge. Cocktails are sipped on the beautiful terraces. *112 Raeburn Place | Stockbridge | tel. 0131 3 32 70 00 | www.theraeburn.com*

Motel One: Tweed meets design? A good match here

STAY CENTRAL
(114 A3) *(ᗰ F5)*

Anyone who likes the idea of staying in an almost 400-year-old guild building in the middle of Edinburgh's Old Town, with contrastingly modern rooms, and mixing with the locals in the down-to-earth and lively hotel bar, won't go wrong with this affordable 3-star hotel. *37 rooms | 139 Cowgate | Old Town | tel. 0131 6 22 68 01 | www.staycentral. co.uk*

INSIDER TIP STEVENSON HOUSE
(109 E5) *(ᗰ D4)*

The author Robert Louis Stevenson (1850–94) lived here from the age of six; today it's a rather exclusive retreat. The only double room has an antique four-poster bed while the breakfast is more in keeping with our times and includes sourdough bread and muesli – the lady of the house is German. The Georgian townhouse also has two single rooms. *3 rooms | 17 Heriot Row | New Town | tel. 01315 56 18 96 | www.stevenson-house.co.uk*

53 FREDERICK STREET (109 E5) *(ᗰ E4)*

This guesthouse (breakfast is included) in a Georgian house in the centre of the New Town offers traditional elegance and large rooms. Peaceful surroundings, attentive and friendly hosts. *6 rooms | 53 Frederick Street | New Town | tel. 01312 26 27 52 | www.53frederickstreet.com*

BALMORE HOUSE (113 E5) *(ᗰ D7)*

Cheerful, immaculate guesthouse with several large rooms a good ten minutes from West End. Victorian Balmore House is decorated in the British style with thick carpets and papered walls while the affiliated neighbouring *Bowmore House* has a Scandinavian touch with wooden floors and light-coloured furniture. A substantial breakfast is included in the price. *7 rooms | 34 Gilmore Place | Old Town | tel. 0131 2 2113 31 | short.travel/edi23*

CLAREMONT (110 A2) *(ᗰ F2)*

Two Georgian houses were joined to create a hotel with high, light-filled rooms that are not over-furnished. Lovely area in the northern part of the New Town. *24 rooms | 14–15 Claremont Crescent | tel. 0131 5 56 14 87 | www.claremont.edin burghhotell.com*

FREDERICK HOUSE
(109 E5) *(𝒸𝓊 E4)*

Former offices were converted to create the rooms – most of them spacious – of this five-storey Georgian New Town hotel. Small bathrooms. Top residential location and tasty à-la-carte breakfast in the restaurant on the other side of the street. *44 rooms | 42 Frederick Street | New Town | tel. 0131 2 26 19 99 | www.frederickhouse hotel.com*

MOTEL ONE EDINBURGH-PRINCES
(114 A1) *(𝒸𝓊 F4)*

Budget hotel with style and a central location by Waverley Station – what's not to like? You will forget the cool functionality of the 140 small rooms in the social foyer, where quotes from design history are blended cheerfully and eclectically (tweed upholstered Jacobsen chairs). Affordable postmodernism. *10–15 Princes Street | New Town | tel. 0131 5 50 92 20 | www.motelone.com*

PLAYFAIR HOUSE
(110 C4) *(𝒸𝓊 G3)*

This wonderfully located B&B on the north side of green Calton Hill and not far from *Playhouse* (see p. 73) and the Broughton quarter is in a Georgian house and was until recently Hotel Twenty. The interior has been lovingly renovated. The small rooms are pretty, the breakfast is good. Very special food (local ingredients, creative cuisine) is on offer directly opposite in INSIDER TIP *The Gardener's Cottage (tel. 0131 6 77 02 44 | www. thegardenerscottage.co | Moderate)*, an old cottage framed by vegetable beds.

11 rooms | 20 Leopold Place/London Road | New Town | tel. 0131 5 56 11 31 | www.hoteltwenty.co.uk

STRAVEN GUEST HOUSE
(117 D1) *(𝒸𝓊 0)*

This small, homely guesthouse is located in Portobello, Edinburgh's sandy beach. You will enjoy a tasty breakfast and pleasant, not too plush, rooms and fresh sea air. The bus takes a good 20 minutes to reach Princes Street. *4 rooms | 3 Brunstone Road North | tel. 0131 69 55 80 | short.travel/edi20 | buses 113, 124*

LOW BUDGET

There are a large number of hostel beds in Edinburgh. The *Belford Hostel (98 dormitory beds, 7 small rooms | from £12/person | 6–8 Douglas Gardens | tel. 0131 2 25 62 09)* in Dean Village is a former church with a house bar. The five-star *Smartcity Hostel (606 beds | £12/person, double room £57 | 50 Blackfriars Street | tel. 0131 5 24 19 89)* is enormous, modern, and in the heart of the Old Town. It also has bicycle and luggage storage facilities.

The *Eurolodge (100 beds, including 4 double rooms | £15/person | 25 Palmerston Place | tel. 0131 2 20 51 41)* in the West End offers Georgian architecture and a past history as a hospital: that's why some of the rooms have as many as 20 beds.

You will often find very attractive last-minute offers for the expensive hotels on *www.short.travel/edi21;* cheap B & Bs on *bedinbedbreak fastedinburgh.*

DISCOVERY TOURS

① EDINBURGH AT A GLANCE

START: ① Valvona & Crolla Caffè Bar
END: ⑲ Royal Oak

Distance:
➡ 9.6 km/6 miles

1 day
Walking time
(without stops)
3 hours

COSTS: admission, food and snacks incl. whisky purchase £40–50
WHAT TO PACK: A hip flask to fill up (for those who like whisky)

IMPORTANT TIPS: The ① **Valvona & Crolla Caffè Bar** opens at 8:30am

Welcome to Edinburgh's two "Old Towns" – a World Heritage Site. Explore both the mundane and medieval faces of the city on a stroll through the New and Old Towns. Go shopping en route and discover what the city has to offer at night.

Would you like to explore the places that are unique to this city? Then the Discovery Tours are just the thing for you – they include terrific tips for stops worth making, breathtaking places to visit, selected restaurants and fun activities. It's even easier with the Touring App: download the tour with map and route to your smartphone using the QR Code on pages 2/3 or from the website address in the footer below – and you'll never get lost again even when you're offline.

TOURING APP

○

→ p. 2/3

08:30am Start your tour with a cappuccino and an Italian-style breakfast in the hip Italian café **❶ Valvona & Crolla** → p. 52 located in the New Town, surrounded by Georgian and Neo-classical architecture.

❶ Valvona & Crolla ☕

09:30am Turn to the south, with Calton Hill→ p. 41 on your left. Walk along Leith Walk and at York Place, head west to the **❷ National Portrait Gallery** → p. 46. Behind the neo-Gothic façade you will see a "who's who" of his-

❷ National Portrait Gallery 🏛

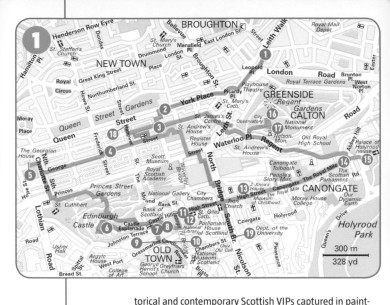

torical and contemporary Scottish VIPs captured in paintings, photographs and even videos.

❸ St Andrew Square 🛍

11:00am Two blocks further south, **❸ St Andrew Square → p. 58 opens up at the end of a small side street on the other side of Queen Street.** Since Edinburgh's political upgrading, this large square – location of the iconic department store **Harvey Nichols → p. 60** – has developed into a real magnet for shoppers. Now **wander westwards** while window shopping along **❹ George Street → p. 62** with its

❹ George Street 🛍

rows of brand-name stores. In dramatic contrast, you'll notice on your left the skyline of the medieval Old Town. In front of you is the Georgian **Charlotte Square → p. 42** designed by Robert Adams in 1791 and now home to the head of government, who resides in No. 6. Number 7 belongs to the National Trust for Scotland preservation society and is a museum called **❺ Georgian House → p. 43**. Immerse yourself in the perfectly restored 200-year-old household of a wealthy family.

❺ Georgian House 🏛

12:30pm Go south, crossing Princes Street, and take a picturesque stroll uphill for 1 km (just over half a mile) through the east side of Princes Street Gardens → p. 43 to **❻ Edinburgh Castle → p. 30**. Make sure you schedule around one hour for the castle visit.

❻ Edinburgh Castle 🏰

`01:30pm` **Head down Royal Mile → p. 35 to the Old Town → p. 28 at the bottom.** Is your stomach starting to rumble? **7 The Grain Store → p. 57** in the picturesque **Victoria Street, five minutes down the Mile,** serves delicious food within its old stone walls. On a full stomach, it's now time for a spot of shopping in the Old Town: **Right next door** you can fill up your hip flask at the **8 Whisky Shop → p. 65** for you to sip later while watching the evening sunset on Calton Hill. **Only a further 100 m (110 yards) downhill, you'll come across Grassmarket → p. 29** and the cult second-hand store **9 Armstrong & Son → p. 62** and just **a few steps further east** the famous hat shop **10 Fabhatrix → p. 62.**

`03:30pm` **Back on Victoria Street return to the 11 Royal Mile**, an endless celebration of Scottish myths and tartan kitsch – but there are also many highlights definitely worth visiting such as **12 St Giles Cathedral → p. 38** – climb up to the roof for an amazing view! – and **13 John Knox House → p. 33.** **Then continue down the Mile and try a Turkish mocha at Café Truva** (daily. | 251–253 Canongate | tel. 0131 5 56 95 24) The modern **14 Scottish Parliament → p. 37** next to the majestic **15 Palace of Holyroodhouse → p. 35 is located at the east end of the Mile.**

`07:00pm` Sunset and the twilight hour now beckon. **Wander from the end of Princes Street onto the grassy lava bump that is 16 Calton Hill → p. 41.** At the top of the hill, you'll discover many strange monuments including the columns of the unfinished **17 National Monument → p. 42.** At the right time of year and weather permitting, you can enjoy the fabulous view of the city's skyline and castle at sunset – and sip whisky from your hip flask while you do so. Sláinte!

`08:00pm` Turn back **in the direction of New Town** to find a restaurant for the evening. **It takes around a quarter of an hour on foot along Princes Street to reach 18 The Dogs → p. 53** which serves affordable, hearty and traditional British cuisine in a bustling and vivacious setting.

`09:30pm` **Walk along North Bridge back to the Old Town and head for the rustic pub 19 Royal Oak → p. 72** to enjoy a beer and folk music in true Edinburgh style: Be prepared, the evening could go well into the night!

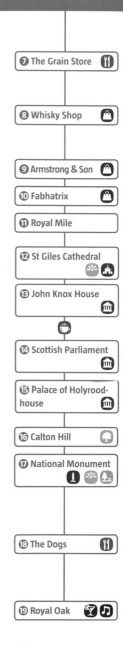

7 The Grain Store

8 Whisky Shop

9 Armstrong & Son

10 Fabhatrix

11 Royal Mile

12 St Giles Cathedral

13 John Knox House

14 Scottish Parliament

15 Palace of Holyroodhouse

16 Calton Hill

17 National Monument

18 The Dogs

19 Royal Oak

IDYLLIC STROLL ALONG THE WATER OF LEITH

START: ❶ Raeburn Place END: ❽ St Cuthbert's Churchyard	4–5 hours Walking time (without stops) 2 hours
Distance: ➡ 6 km/3.7 miles	

COSTS: £5–10 for picnic supplies	

IMPORTANT TIPS: more information at *www.waterofleith.org.uk*

Not many visitors to Edinburgh think about following the Water of Leith Walkway as it winds its way through rural countryside around the city. But it's well worth exploring! Go down into the small wooded gorge in hip Stockbridge, wander through Dean Village and you'll soon leave the hustle and bustle of the Royal Mile behind you. The entire walkway is around 20 km (12 miles) long, but there are many places along the way where you can interrupt it.

❶ Raeburn Place

❷ St Bernard's Well

❸ Dean Bridge

Art, not only on the inside:
Scottish Gallery of Modern Art

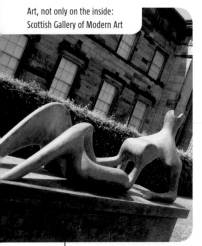

10:00am Your tour begins at ❶ **Raeburn Place** → p. 64, a street with many small shops. An old barber's, a fishmonger's and second-hand shops invite you to go window-shopping and rummage around. You can also find some deliciously sweet temptations for a picnic at **Patisserie Madeleine** (house no. 27b). With your bag full of goodies, **stroll down to Kerr-Street Bridge where you then make your way down to the banks of the Water of Leith.** Once there, you will be in green surroundings. Wrought-iron fencing frame the banks often frequented by blue kingfishers. You can catch a fleeting glimpse of the old villas up on Upper **Dean Terrace** through the treetops. **Stroll along the east bank following the signposts to the galleries and, a few minutes later, you will be standing in front of ❷ St Bernard's Well**. The small temple with the figure of Hygeia, the Greek goddess of cleanliness, marks the place where an ancient spring once stood and is the perfect spot to enjoy your pastries. **A little further on, the slender supports of ❸ Dean Bridge soar into the sky. The route takes you along Miller Row, along rural lanes with half-timbered houses.**

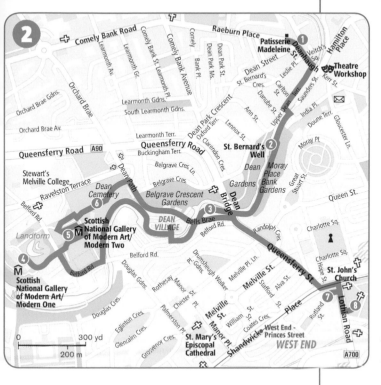

Mills and bread ovens were standing here almost 1,000 years ago. The depictions of the paddles used to remove bread from the ovens painted on some house walls are a sign of the baker's guild. **If you now saunter along Hawthornbank Lane, you'll be treated to a panoramic view of the stone walls of Dean Village → p. 46** – a perfect photo opportunity.

11:30am Cross the small bridge and climb up out of the gorge after the river bend to reach the two classical gallery temples on Belford Road. The **4 Scottish National Gallery of Modern Art One → p. 48** and **5 Scottish National Gallery of Modern Art Two → p. 48** exhibit the most exciting modern art, and as admission is free, you should consider taking a break for a short visit and enjoy a cup of tea served with a piece of cake. On no account should you miss the sculptures by Moore and Gormley, and the landscape art by Charles Jencks.

4 Scottish National Gallery of Modern Art One

5 Scottish National Gallery of Modern Art Two

⑥ Dean Cemetery

`01:30pm` Your journey home starts behind the second gallery: Cross the beautiful ⑥ INSIDER TIP Dean Cemetery and when you leave, turn right along Dean Path. Once you have crossed the water, you'll reach Dean Bridge again down Bell's Brae. Head south-east along the main road to Queensferry Street which merges into the west end of Princes Street. Half way down Queensferry Street you will be confronted with an outstanding example of Edinburgh's different architectural styles: **Melville Street on the right** is characterised by a row of Georgian townhouse façades with a stylised Gothic church looming up in contrast behind them. **After about 200 m (250 yards), you'll reach the splendid bar ⑦ The Huxley → p. 77** in the Rutland Hotel, well worth popping in for a drink. You are treated to the best view of **Edinburgh Castle → p. 30** from **⑧ St Cuthbert's Churchyard → p. 45!**

⑦ The Huxley 🍸

⑧ St Cuthbert's Churchyard 🌼 💬

③ LITERARY TOUR ON THE TRAIL OF PROSE AND POETRY

START: ❶ James Court END: ❿ The Elephant House	2–3 hours Walking time (without stops) 40 min
Distance: ➡ 3 km/1.9 miles	

COSTS: £22 admission plus food & drink in pubs & cafés
WHAT TO PACK: reading material from Burns, Stevenson, Rowling and co. – if you wish to do some reading along the way

IMPORTANT TIPS: You can find more information at *www.edinburgh literarypubtour.co.uk* and *www.edinburghbookloverstour.com*

It is impossible to overlook the places where prose and poetry were written in a city that Unesco named the first World City of Literature in 2004. Stroll through the labyrinth of old lanes – called *closes* and *wynds* – that branch off the Royal Mile. Take a couple of hours to track down around 300 years of literature. If you take this tour in the evening, definitely stop off at one or two of the pubs on the way.

❶ James Court

`02:00pm` The walk begins at ❶ James Court. The inner courtyard is surrounded by pretty residential buildings – this is where the journalist and author James Boswell (1740–95) rented a flat. He had to leave his wife and child behind when he went to look for a publisher for his works in the city. To his dismay, he was forced to work in the legal profession and 'rewarded' himself with a free and easy nightlife. There were many pubs in this district for Boswell to choose from, such as the cellar pub ❷ **Jolly Judge** *(7 James Court)*. Besides meeting Voltaire and Rousseau, one of the highlights of his literary ambitions was his encounter with England's most celebrated intellectual, Samuel Johnson in Edinburgh in 1763. The famous lexicographer – and author of the first English dictionary – subsequently set out on an arduous trip to the Outer Hebrides with Boswell in August 1773 which was to last several months. INSIDER TIP▶ The books written by the two men still make great reading today and are regarded as famous travel literature. Take your first pub break here. **Head back to the Royal Mile, take a left and enter a six-storey residential building** from the 17th century, ❸ **Gladstone's Land** *(April–Dec. daily 10am–5pm | admission £7)*. It belongs to the National Trust and gives an insight into how the wealthy merchant Gladstone and his tenants once resided. **Then return to the Mile where you will reach the next street on your left hand side: Lady Stair's Close.** This is where the Scottish national poet Robert Burns (1759–96) spent a winter. Burns had just written his first volume in Scots, influenced by the young, extremely talented Robert Fergusson (1750–74), whose striding bronze figure has been erected in the lower section of the Royal Mile. Burns incorporated Old Town characters such as market women and pub owners into his poetry. The small ❹ **The Writers' Museum** → p. 39 in Lady Stair's Close is devoted to Edinburgh's most influential writers. Here you can buy a volume of Burns' verse in Scots dialect, which is in fact not too hard to understand.

03:30pm **Back on the Mile, turn left. At the first street junction, you have another opportunity for a pub break.** It is named after a joiner and city councillor who stole from his customers at night using duplicate keys: ❺ **Deacon Brodie's Tavern**. Brodie had his joiner's workshop at **Brodie's Close**, which is the street diagonally across from the Mile. In 1788, Brodie was hung from the gallows which he had made so efficiently himself as a joiner a few years before. 100 years later, Robert Louis Stevenson turned Brodie's story into his famous novel about Dr. Jekyll alias Mr Hyde. The same junction is dominated by the sitting statue of the philosopher David Hume (1711–76). Hume was a political economist, civil-rights theoretician and an acquaintance of the market-economy philosopher Adam

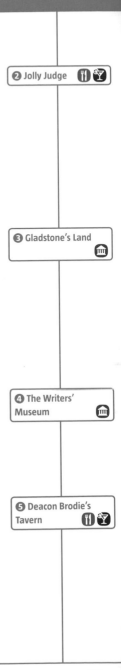

❷ Jolly Judge

❸ Gladstone's Land

❹ The Writers' Museum

❺ Deacon Brodie's Tavern

⑥ Heart of Midlothian ❗

⑦ St Giles Cathedral ⌂

⑧ The Real Mary King's Close 🏛

Smith, a scholar of the Scottish Enlightenment. **Back on the Mile, which is called Lawnmarket here, you'll come to the point** where Brodie was left hanging, Tollbooth Prison, that is now only marked by the so-called **⑥ Heart of Midlothian → p. 32** in the pavement. Here you'll also stumble across the name of Walter Scott, whose popularity initiated Scotland's tourism. **From the Heart of Midlothian, go right to ⑦ St Giles Cathedral → p. 38** to see how Edinburgh honours its writers of life on the city's streets: Burns has been given a memorial window and Robert Louis Stevenson is remembered with a sculptured plaque.

04:00pm You should not miss two other lanes opposite the church. On the left, the name of **Advocate's Close** reminds us that Stevenson, Scott and Boswell were all lawyers. **⑧ The Real Mary King's Close → p. 35** gives an impression of how things were in the year of the plague in 1645 when the street and its people were walled in. A tour of the two closes shows how the inhabitants of the Old Town fought against hunger, filth and disease. **Now head 50 m (55 yards) down the Mile and enter Old Fishmarket Close on your right. Then cross Cowgate, the road that runs parallel to the Mile to the south, and turn into Guthrie Street opposite.** Walter Scott was born here while the street was still named College Wynd. **At the south end**

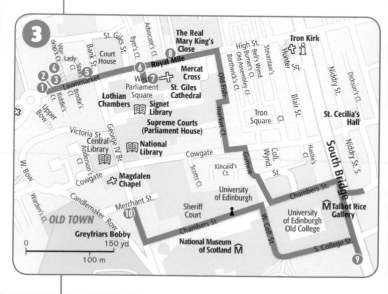

Harry Potter fans (and others) meet here: The Elephant House

of Guthry, turn left and go over South Bridge to **Infirmary Street,** where Scott attended the Royal High School, today a university building. This was the site of the Old Royal Infirmary where the writer William Ernest Henley convalesced for almost two years after undergoing a foot amputation due to tuberculosis. He became the model for the pirate with the wooden leg, Long John Silver, in Stevenson's "Treasure Island". Stevenson visited his friend regularly in his sick bed. They wrote the drama "Deacon Brodie" together in 1880, which became the precursor of Stevenson's famous novel "Strange Case of Dr Jekyll and Mr Hyde". **Back on South Bridge, turn left and after a minute you'll reach the café ❾ Spoon → p. 52** – a plaque outside notes that J. K. Rowling wrote some chapters of "Harry Potter" here, when it was still called Nicholson's Café. Take a look inside and maybe drink a coffee to Rowling on the first floor. Another chapter in the Potter story was written only 500 m (550 yards) west of here in the café ❿ **The Elephant House** *(21 George IV Bridge | www.elephanthouse. biz)*. Go to the café's website to read INSIDER TIP an interview with J. K. Rowling to get in the mood for your visit.

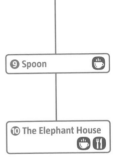

❾ Spoon

❿ The Elephant House

4 OVER THE VOLCANO

START: ❶ The Scottish Parliament
END: ❼ Dr Neil's Garden

4–5 hours
Walking time
(without stops)
a good 2 hours

Distance: easy
➡ 5.6 km/3.5 mi · ‖ Height: 300 m/656 ft

COSTS: pub food and drinks
WHAT TO PACK: sturdy footwear and rainwear

Similar to Rome and Lisbon, Edinburgh has seven volcanic hills. But only here does the terrain invite you on a tour with a Highland feeling – right at the heart of the city! After the steep ascent to Arthur's Seat, you will be rewarded for your efforts by a view of an idyllic lake and a beer in Scotland's oldest watering hole.

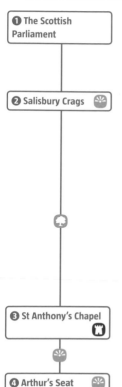

❶ The Scottish Parliament

❷ Salisbury Crags 🌳

❸ St Anthony's Chapel 🏛

❹ Arthur's Seat 🌳

`12:00pm` ❶ **The Scottish Parliament** is the starting point. **After just 220 m (240 yards) to the south, you'll reach Queen's Drive,** which winds around the entire massif. **Keep to the left of the drive and turn off right onto a mountain path after approx. 100 m (110 yards): Radical Road.**

Stage one takes you up a steep path below ❷ **Salisbury Crags,** a procession of 46 m (150 ft) high basalt columns that can be seen from far away. You will be rewarded with splendid views over the city. **Just before you return to Queen's Drive, turn left, and then left again after approx. 50 m (55 yards), to now follow, in the opposite direction to before, a path called Volunteer's Walk towards the north. You are now walking through a terrace above the crags.** By now you will have left the city far behind and a highland hiking feeling will have taken over.

`01:00pm` Leave the damp and boggy area, Hunter's Bog, to your right: the view sweeps over the city to the Firth. **After another 300 m (330 yards), turn right this time, off the path that curves left, just before reaching Queen's Drive once again.** Your destination is the remains of ❸ **St Anthony's Chapel** *(short.travel/edi3)*, towering 200 m (220 yards) to the east, which is dramatically exposed above St Margaret's Loch. **Follow the lightly-worn paths to this elevation.** Take a moment to enjoy the magnificent panoramic view. **Walk towards the south again, straight towards the gentle volcanic peak of ❹ Arthur's Seat → p. 29** 251 m (823 ft). **You will reach the summit**

around 1 km (0.6 mi) beyond the ruins. Now you are standing 170 m (185 yards) above the start of the route. The view to the Firth of Forth in the distance is amazing.

03:00pm **For the descent, aim for Dunsapie Loch 500 m (550 yards) to the east** – follow one of the trails down to the car park on Queen's Drive at the south end of the loch. The water of ❺ **Duddingston Loch** sparkles a good 200 m (220 yards) further south. **If you turn off Queen's Drive to the left after 50 m (55 yards), you will reach the The Causeway,** a little road where refreshment beckons in the shape of the ❻ **Sheep Heid Inn** → p. 69 Even Mary, Queen of Scots once stopped for a restorative here in the oldest pub in Scotland. **A few steps further is a meditative and inspiring botanic enclave with free admission:** ❼ **Dr Neil's Garden** *(www.drneilsgarden.co.uk)*. Enjoy the INSIDER TIP splendid view of the back of the volcano. **From the lake, bus 42 takes you back to the city.**

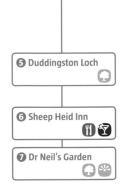

❺ Duddingston Loch

❻ Sheep Heid Inn

❼ Dr Neil's Garden

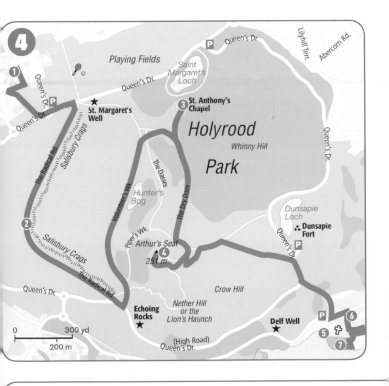

TRAVEL WITH KIDS

Children can have a thrilling time in Edinburgh. The tours through the *Dungeons* chamber of horrors at Waverley Station, however are for hardened teenagers accompanied by adults. The evening *Ghost Tours* through the lanes of the city are less scary, and the actors' costumes are an extra bonus. The city has of course many other less hair-raising activities to offer.

DEEP SEA WORLD ●
(116 C1) (*ℳ 0*)
A conveyor belt takes visitors through a kind of aquarium with sharks, rays, schools of colourful fish and seals. INSIDER TIP With a supervised diving session for beginners, you experience 3-m (10-ft) sharks and rays in their own element (£95–185). Online booking 48 hours in advance saves 25 percent. *Mon–Fri 10am–4pm, Sat, Sun 10am–5pm | admission £15, children 3–12 £11 | North Queensferry | www.deepsea world.com | Fife Circle Line from Waverley or Haymarket*
The most fascinating aspect of the almost 10-mile excursion to North Queensferry – at least for parents – will probably be the train journey across the Firth of Forth Bridge, the most famous cantilever bridge in the world. You can include a

45-minute boat trip from South Queensferry directly under the bridge *(Feb–Oct)* and spend one-and-a-half hours on *Inchcolm Island.* There are wonderful abbey ruins on the island and many sea birds and seals on the shore from April/May.

EDINBURGH ZOO
(116 C2) (*ℳ 0*)
The landscape of the hilly zoo is really beautiful. INSIDER TIP And there are Great Pandas. Start your visit by taking the shuttle to the top of the zoo and then wander down the hill past the koalas, rhinoceroses and other animals. Children love the penguin parade *(April–Aug 2:15pm).* Don't set off without a packed lunch! Pre-book online. *April–Sept daily 9am–6pm, Oct and March daily 9am–5pm, Nov–Feb daily 10am–4pm | admission £19, children over the age of 3 £14.55 | 134 Corstorphine Road | Murrayfield | www.edinburghzoo. org.uk | buses 12, 21, 22, 26, 31, 38, 100*

HORROR TOURS
Sooner or later, somebody will thrust a colourful flyer into your hand and entice you into the dark corners of town. Quite a few amateur actors make their living from scaring the wits out of visitors for a

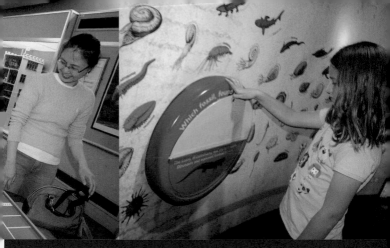

Pandas at the zoo, glacier tours in a museum – and some ghosts in the evening. Tablets and phones won't be missed

couple of hours. A bit like a historical ghost train, professionally performed with costumes and makeup – not for the faint-hearted but exciting for bright kids. *Mercat Walking Tours (children £8, adults £13 | tel. 0131 225 54 45 | www.mercat tours.com); City of the Dead Tours (from £11 | tel. 0131 225 90 44 | www.blackhart. uk.com); Witchery Tours (children £7.50, adults £10 | tel. 0131 225 67 45 | www. witcherytours.com)*

MUSEUM OF CHILDHOOD
(114 B2) (*Ⓜ G5*)

Parents and their children immerse themselves in the history of youth and discover what kids played with before the advent of the Smartphone. Wonderful exhibits in the world's first childhood museum, renovated in 2018, show how kids grew up in Edinburgh. *Mon–Sat 10am–5pm, Sun noon–5pm | free admission | 42 High Street | Old Town | www. edinburghmuseums.org.uk/venues/mu seum-of-childhood*

OUR DYNAMIC EARTH ★
(115 D2) (*Ⓜ H5*)

The science museum in a gigantic tent construction below Arthur's Seat is a real hit with schoolchildren. The journey through time begins with the Big Bang, 14 billion years ago. Earthquake simulator, volcano eruption scenario, a virtual trip through the world of glaciers and the centre of the Earth. Global climatic scenarios can be investigated in the "Future" section. The affiliated *Earthscape Scotland Gallery* explains the geology of the country; there is a fine example outside – the gallery is next to the volcanic peak, Arthur's Seat. The geology lesson is also intended to be an homage to the Edinburgh resident James Hutton (1726–97), who is considered the founder of that particular science. The great scenario also hosts events and workshops. *Nov–March Wed–Sun 10am–5:30pm, otherwise daily 10am–5:30pm | admission £15, children under 15 £9.50 | 4 Holyrood Road | www.dynamicearth.co.uk*

FESTIVALS & EVENTS

Things really come to life in August when several festivals attract visitors. Further information under *www.eventsedinburgh.org.uk* and *www.edinburghfestivalcity.com*.

EVENTS

JANUARY
25 Jan: Robert Burns' birthday is celebrated in restaurants with haggis and whisky, and his verses (on haggis) recited on *Burns Night*.

APRIL
The 2-week *International Science Festival* (*www.sciencefestival.co.uk*) focuses on technology and science.
Last week of April until first week of May: The INSIDER TIP *TradFest* celebrates Scottish culture in music and literature.
30 April: The INSIDER TIP *Beltane Fire Festival* is a Celtic mega-party on Calton Hill. More than 12,000 people welcome the summer every year with bonfires and drums – a great way to dance into May.

MAY
End of May: The *Imaginate Festival* (*www.imaginate.org/uk/festival*) is Great Britain's largest theatre festival for children and young people, but there are also many adults in the audience.

JUNE
Second half of June: The 4-day *Royal Highland Show* (*www.royalhighlandshow.org*), held near the airport, is Scotland's largest agricultural show.
Mid-June: Stars like Sean Connery, Tilda Swinton and Robert Carlyle are often patrons at the twelve-day *Edinburgh International Film Festival* (*www.edfilmfest.org.uk*)

JULY
Mid-July: The *Edinburgh Jazz & Blues Festival* (*www.edinburghjazzfestival.com*) lasts ten days.

AUGUST/SEPTEMBER
The *Edinburgh International Festival* (*3 weeks from mid-Aug, www.eif.co.uk*) with a classic programme and the *Edinburgh Festival Fringe* (*3 weeks in August | www.edfringe.com, www.freefestival.co.uk*) with countless theatre and comedy productions are considered the world's largest cultural events.
The *Edinburgh Military Tattoo* (*3 weeks in Aug | www.edinburgh-tattoo.co.uk*) with the castle as its backdrop is the

Edinburgh is a stage for cultural events throughout the year: mystic festivals, theatre, music and even one for the haggis

most spectacular military-band festival worldwide.

2nd half of August: The *Edinburgh International Book Festival* (*www.edbookfest. co.uk*) with more than 800 events.

The *Edinburgh Art Festival* (*4 weeks in Aug and Sept | www.edinburghartfestival. com*) in the city's museums and galleries is a relatively new event.

SEPTEMBER

At the start of September, world music is celebrated at the *Edinburgh Mela* (*www. edinburgh-mela.co.uk*) in Leith.

OCTOBER

Last week in Oct: Scots love telling stories and celebrate this aspect of their culture at the *Scottish International Storytelling Festival* (*www.tracscotland.org*).

DECEMBER

Edinburgh's Christmas is Great Britain's largest Christmas market with an ice skating rink; held in Princes Street Gardens.

29 Dec–1 Jan: The popular three- to four-day New Year's celebration is known as *Hogmanay* (*www.edinburghhogmanay. org*). The highlight is the New Year's Eve street party (admission fee!) where tens of thousands celebrate throughout the city.

NATIONAL HOLIDAYS

If Christmas or New Year's Day fall on Sat or Sun, Mon is a public holiday.

1 January	*New Year's Day*
2 January	*2nd January*
March/April	*Good Friday*
last Monday in May	*Spring Bank Holiday*
first Monday in August	*Summer Bank Holiday*
30 November	*St Andrews Day*
25 December	*Christmas Day*
26 December	*Boxing Day*

LINKS, BLOGS, APPS & MORE

en.wikipedia.org/wiki/Portal: Scotland History, politics, geography and things to do – here you can find the answers to many a question about Scotland!

www.edinburghspotlight.com This website publishes tips, reviews and blogs about culture, food, children, access for the disabled, sport and daily excursions. All you need to know about the capital city, and up-to-date – take a look at it!

www.visitscotland.com/see-do/attractions/tv-film Shows film and TV locations throughout Scotland. Apart from that, this official tourism site has lots of information on the country an the city

www.edinburghfestivals.co.uk The official Edinburgh festivals website for tickets, news and reviews to help you plan a trip to the capital and make the most of your stay

www.edinburghwhiskyblog.com or new kids on the whisky blog: Two locals in their mid-twenties create a stir in the world of the whisky connoisseur through their blog. If malt ever needed a breath of fresh air, it would get it here. A new, charming facet of the tasty brew

www.guardian.co.uk/edinburgh Up-to-the-minute journalistic blog on matters affecting the capital city from one of England's leading daily papers. At it's very best!

citycyclingedinburgh.info/bbpress Forum for cyclists in the city

short.travel/edi25 The Edinburgh page on this great website provides meticulous information about a number of buildings, green areas and festivals. The "Late Availabilities" link lists last-minute offers for accommdation

www.edinburghetiquette.co.uk Charming blog on design, shopping, fashion and food – up-to-date with an archive

Regardless of whether you are still researching your trip or already in Edinburgh: these addresses will provide you with more information, videos and networks to make your holiday even more enjoyable

www.audioboom.com/thisismyedinburgh Six audio interviews revealing personal perspectives on Edinburgh

www.citysocializer.com/edinburgh/meet-friends Even if you don't intend to move to Edinburgh – this is where you can come into contact with many people with a great variety of interests

VIDEOS

short.travel/edi26 Scots love story-telling. The video will really get you in the mood

www.youtube.com/watch?v=WymV2Bah1Rk Great amateur video portrait of his home town made by a native of Edinburgh

conventionedinburgh.com/video-gallery.html Four professional videos on the official site of the Edinburgh Convention Bureau

www.camvista.com/scotland/edinburgh/histedin_streaming.php3 The webcam portal shows various camera angles of the city; good for an up-to-date check on the weather

www.edinburghfestivals.co.uk/video Film about Edinburgh's Festivals of the past years

Ian Rankin's Edinburgh You can follow crime writer Ian Rankin through his home-town with this free app. Explanatory and enlightening

APPS

Urbanspoon What is being served these days in Edinburgh's restaurants and how does it taste? This app for iPhone, iPad and iPod lets you know

EdinBus The Edinburgh bus timetable with many extra functions as a free app

City of the Dead Tours: Haunted Edinburgh The App on enchanted and haunted corners of the city – for Android and iOS

Lit Long Edinburgh Constantly updated App with hundreds of tips on literary locations

TRAVEL TIPS

ARRIVAL

✈ Direct flights to Edinburgh: from Belfast, Birmingham, Bristol, Cardiff, Chicago, Cork, Dublin, East Midlands, Exeter, Ireland West/Knock, Jersey, Kirkwall, Liverpool, London (City, Gatwick, Heathrow, Luton, Stansted), Manchester, New York, Newquay, Norwich, Orlando, Shannon, Southampton, Stornoway, Toronto, Wick, e.g. with *flybe (www.flybe. com)* or *easyjet (www.easyjet.com)*. Edinburgh Airport *(www.edinburghairport. com)* is located around eight miles west of the city centre. The bus trip to Princes Street and Waverley Station takes about half an hour. *Airlink 100* operates around the clock; every ten minutes during the day and every 15 minutes at night; the fare is £4.50. The night bus N22 travels to the city and Leith between 0:15am and 4am for £3. Mini-buses start from the car park and will bring you to your doorstep in town for £32. A tram to the city leaves every seven minutes (travel time 30 minutes, fare £5).
Skylink double-decker buses *(short.travel/edi28)* operate to north Edinburgh (200) and west and south Edinburgh (300). If several people travel together, a taxi from around £29 is another alternative.

🚆 There is at least one direct train to Edinburgh every hour from Kings Cross Station in London *(www.mytrain ticket.co.uk)*. The journey usually takes around 4 hours 30 min; ticket prices vary from £40 to £240. The journey from Glasgow Central Station to Edinburgh Waverley Station *(www.scotrail.co.uk)* takes about one hour, the price of an open return starts at £13.

⛴ From Ireland, several companies run regular services (even up to eight times a day) between the Emerald Isle and Scotland. The routes between Belfast and Stranraer (a 2 hour crossing), Belfast and Cairnryan (2 hours 15 min) and Larne to Troon (2) are probably the most interesting. Alternatively there are ferries to North Wales and Liverpool from Dun Laoghaire and Cork, for example. Compare prices and times: Irish Ferries *(www.irishferries.com)*, Stena Lines *(www. stenaline.com)*, Brittany Ferries *(www. brittanyferries.com)*.

RESPONSIBLE TRAVEL

It doesn't take a lot to be environmentally friendly whilst travelling. Don't just think about your carbon footprint whilst flying to and from your holiday destination but also about how you can protect nature and culture abroad. As a tourist it is especially important to respect nature, look out for local products, cycle instead of driving, save water and much more. If you would like to find out more about eco-tourism please visit: *www.ecotourism.org*

BANKS & CREDIT CARDS

It is easy to withdraw money from cash dispensers all over the city using your EC card. Shops, hotels, restaurants and most pubs accept standard credit cards. Banks are open from *9am to 5pm Mon–Fri*, except, of course, on public holidays.

From arrival to weather

CITY TOURS

Edinburgh Bus Tours (www.edinburghtour. com), the public service bus, offers four sightseeing trips in open double-decker buses that start from Waverley Station. "City Sightseeing" trip and the "Majestic Tour" (£15, one hour) provide information in several languages by way of headphones. The "Edinburgh Tour" is accompanied by live commentary. The "3 Bridges Tour" (£20, 3 hours) takes you through the city and on a boat trip on the Firth of Forth. Most tours are hop-on hop-off and tickets are valid for 24 hours. For a good first overview, try one of the free guided city tours that start at Starbuck's at Tron Kirk on the Royal Mile on the hour between 10am and 3pm and last around 2 hours 30 min. Please book in advance online. A two-hour Castle Tour costs £29, a Pub Crawl Tour of indefinite length £15 plus drinks of course *(www.neweurope tours.eu/edinburgh/en/home#)*. More tours here: www.*edinburghfreetour.com*. *Allen Fosters Book Lovers Tour (www.edin burghbookloverstour.com)* is especially recommended for lovers of literature and an evening pub crawl with two entertainers *(www.edinburghliterarypubtour.com)* is another highlight. The ghost tour market is highly competitive and this often leads to calculated kitsch. The most acceptable of the kind is the *Murder and Mystery Tour* with Adam Lyle, who was hung in 1871 (adults £10, children £8.50 | *75 min* | *www. witcherytours.com).*

CURRENCY

In Edinburgh, the currency is the British pound (GBP) divided into 100 pence.

Don't be surprised: Paper money looks different in Scotland than in the rest of Great Britain but has the same value. You can change your Scottish banknotes for English pounds (or euros) at the airport. You will have problems paying with Scottish currency in England; however, it does work the other way round. Three banks in Scotland print their own notes and there are even Royal Bank of Scotland £1 notes in circulation. The pretty motifs can make bank notes an interesting souvenir for fans of Scotland.

CUSTOMS

The allowance when entering Great Britain from countries outside the European Union, including North America, is: 1 litre of spirits, 200 cigarettes or 100 cigarillos or 50 cigars or 250 g of tobacco, 50 g of perfume or 250 g of eau de toilette and other articles (except gold) to a value of £390. Note that the import of self-defence sprays is prohibited and the import of other weapons requires licences. For more information: *www.hmrc.gov.uk/customs*

ELECTRICITY

230–240 volt alternating current. If you need it, you can buy an adapter for a three-pin plug in Edinburgh or ask at your hotel for one.

EMBASSIES & CONSULATES

CONSULATE OF THE UNITED STATES OF AMERICA
3 Regent Terrace, Edinburgh, EH7 5BW | tel. (44) 131 5 56 83 15 | uk.usembassy.gov/ embassy-consulates/edinburgh

CANADIAN HONORARY CONSULATE
Tel. (44) 770 23 59 916 | www.canadainter national.gc.ca/united_kingdom-royau me_uni/offices-bureaux/edinburgh-edim bourg.aspx?lang=eng

CONSULATE GENERAL OF IRELAND
16 Randolph Crescent | Edinburgh EH3 7TT | tel: (44) 131 2 26 77 11 | www.dfa.ie/irish-consulate/edinburgh/

EMERGENCY SERVICES

Police, fire brigade, emergency doctor: *tel. 999*

HEALTH

For non-UK residents, the European Insurance card issued by your social security office is accepted in hospitals run by the *National Health Service (NHS)* and most doctors. In special cases, you will have to pay directly and submit your bill for refunding when you return home. You can find the nearest hospital on this website: *www.nhs.uk/Service-Search*

INFORMATION IN EDINBURGH

EDINBURGH iCENTRE
3 Princes Street | (*) tel. 0131 473 38 68; Airport Tourist Information Desk | Airport | (*) tel. 0131 4 73 36 90

INTERNET & WIFI

Edinburgh now has a very good network. If you bring your laptop or Internet mobile phone with you, you will be able to surf on the Internet using WiFi in most hotels and an increasing number of bed & breakfasts – usually, free of charge. Many hotels have computer facilities in the lobby or a business centre where you can check your mails and get information. If you do not want to take advantage of these services, there are several Internet cafés in the city.

LEFT LUGGAGE

At the airport, the main Waverley Station and the bus station on St Andrew Square.

SPOTLIGHT ON SPORTS

Football has a much harder time in Edinburgh than in Glasgow: the two more than 130-year-old local clubs *Heart of Midlothian* and *Hibernian* – the Hearts and Hibs for short – just do not whip up the enthusiasm of Celtic and the Rangers to the west. As is the case in Glasgow, the following has something to do with religion: the Hibs are Catholic like Celtic and the Hearts and Rangers are both Protestant. Tickets for the games of the two capital-city clubs start at £20; fans should book in advance via the Internet, e.g. under *www.livefoot-balltickets.com/spl-tickets.html*.
The Scottish National Rugby Team's home games are played in Murray-field during the *Six Nations* Championship – a kind of Rugby Union European Championship. Tickets online at *www.scottishrugby.org,* also for the games of the Edinburgh Rugby Team in the British League.

Pleasant and comfortable: seeing Edinburgh on a guided bus tour

NEWSPAPERS & MAGAZINES

The leading newspaper in the capital is *The Scotsman (www.scotsman.com)*. Here you will find daily tips as well as ticket prices for a number of events in the city. Major international newspapers are also available but not always on the day of publication. The excellent event calendar *The List (www.list.co.uk)* is published every second Thursday. This is where to look, along with the portal *(www.ticket master.co.uk)*, if you want to go out (search for "Edinburgh"). Fans of pop music will like *Is this Music (www.isthismusic. com)*. The quarterly *Chapman (www. chapman-pub.co.uk)* gives information on all the current news in the literary scene.

PERSONAL SAFETY

Edinburgh is a fairly safe city, at night as well as during the day. The typical enter-tainment areas around Cowgate and Tollcross are always very lively at week-ends and you should count on meeting a few exuberant drunks.

BUDGETING

Beer	from £3.00/$ 3.90 *for a pint*
Bus	£1.60/$2.10 *for a single journey*
Fish and chips	from £4.80/$6.30 *for a take-away serving*
Coffee	from £2.20/$2.90 *a cup*
Whisky	from £26/$34 *a bottle*
Cinema	from £9.50/$12.50 *for a ticket*

PHONES & MOBILE PHONES

The dialling code for Edinburgh is 0131. For calls from abroad, dial 0044 (Great Britain) 131. Mobile numbers begin with 077, 078 or 079. 0800 and 0808 numbers are toll-free; premium rate numbers start with 09.

Many telephone boxes operate with a credit card and shops with the BT symbol, such as chemist's, post offices and newsagents, sell phone cards.

Check with you mobile-phone provider to find out which is the most economical roaming partner. If you use a Scottish prepaid card, you will not be charged for incoming calls. Texting is still the least expensive means of communication. If travelling from outside the UK, turn your mobile mailbox off before you leave home as this can cause high costs when you are abroad.

POST

Post offices are open from *9am to 5:30pm, Mon–Fri* and from *9am to noon on Sat*. You can purchase single stamps from post offices *(40 Frederick Street | New Town; 46 St Mary's Street | Old Town)* and booklets with several stamps in shops with the Royal Mail sign. Postcards require a 60p stamp, a letter to the continent £1.17.

PUBLIC TRANSPORT

There is an excellent network of buses *(www.lothianbuses.com)*. A single ticket costs £1.60 for adults, a day ticket £2 for children, £4 for adults. However, the city is small and the distances within the Old Town, New Town, Dean Village and Stockbridge are perfect for walking, which is why we have not included bus lines and stops for the sights in this guide. Trams

WEATHER IN EDINBURGH

	Jan	Feb	March	April	May	June	July	Aug	Sept	Oct	Nov	Dec
Daytime temperatures in °C/°F												
	5/41	6/43	8/46	11/52	14/57	17/63	18/64	18/64	16/61	12/54	9/48	7/45
Nighttime temperatures in °C/°F												
	1/34	1/34	2/36	4/39	6/43	9/48	11/52	11/52	9/48	7/45	4/39	2/36
Sunshine hours/day	2	3	3	5	6	6	5	4	4	3	2	2
Precipitation days/month	13	11	11	11	11	12	13	13	12	13	12	13

☀ Sunshine hours/day ☂ Precipitation days/month

connect the airport with Leith and travel down Princes Street.

The bus driver will only accept the correct change – otherwise buy tickets beforehand from machines at bus stops. If you want to pay for public transport with your Smartphone, you will have to download this App: www.tfeapp.com. It will also inform you when the next bus or tram is due to arrive.

TIME

Greenwich Mean Time; daylight saving time starts and finishes on the same dates as in continental Europe. The North American east coast is five hours behind, the west coast eight hours.

TIPPING

It is usual to tip taxi drivers and in restaurants. Round the bill up by about 10 percent. If the restaurant bill or menu states service charge included, this means that the tip has already been taken into account and it is not necessary to give anything extra. Tipping is not usual in pubs.

WEATHER

The Scots used to call Edinburgh "Auld Reekie" – old smokie. A good 50 years ago, thick smoke poured out of the countless chimneys of the high-rise buildings that were still heated with coal. Today, Edinburgh is almost like a climatic health resort with often dramatic, cloud-framed views of the North Sea that you can admire from the volcanic hills. Sometimes fog – called *haar* – makes its way into the city from April to September; this is caused by warm air condensing over the cold North Sea. Winter is a good time to visit

CURRENCY CONVERTER

$	£	£	$
1	0.68	1	1.47
3	2	3	4.40
5	3.40	5	7.30
13	8.90	13	19
40	27	40	59
75	51	75	110
120	82	120	176
250	170	250	367
500	340	500	734

For current exchange rates see www.xe.com

Edinburgh when, on clear days, the low-lying sun creates a dramatic play of light on the Old Town. And even in the rain, the city retains its special charm.

WEIGHTS & MEASURES

For overseas visitors: officially, Edinburgh (and all of Great Britain) calculates with the metric and decimal systems but the imperial standards are still used in everyday life:

1 inch = 2.54 cm; 1 foot = 30.48 cm; 1 yard = 91.44 cm; 1 mile = 1.609 km; 1 ounce = 28.35 g; 1 pound = 453.59 g; 1 pint = 0.5683 l; 1 gallon = 4.5459 l.

STREET ATLAS

The green line indicates the Discovery Tour "Edinburgh at a glance"
The blue line indicates the other Discovery Tours
All tours are also marked on the pull-out map

Exploring Edinburgh

The map on the back cover shows how the area has been subdivided

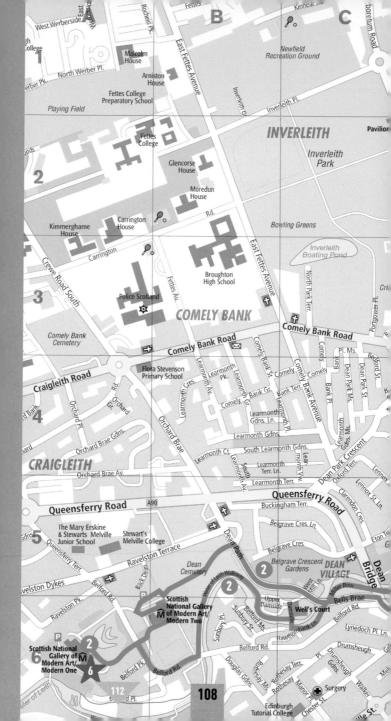

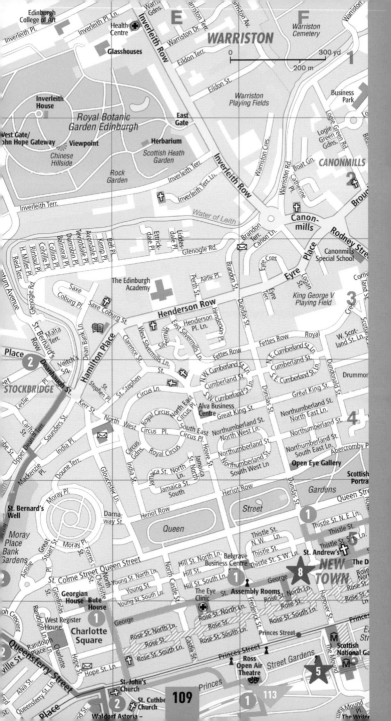

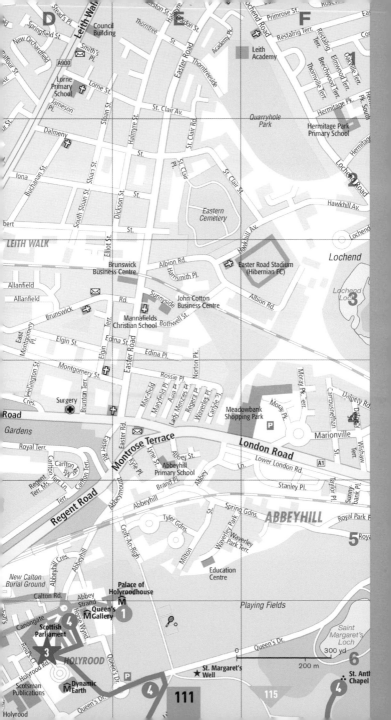

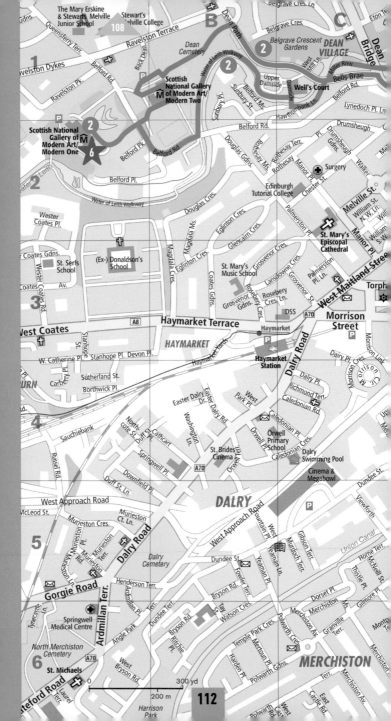

The Mary Erskine & Stewart's Melville Junior School
Stewart's Melville College
108
Queensferry Terr.
Ravelston Terrace
Dean Path
Belgrave Cres. Ln.
Belgrave Cres.
Eton Te
C
1
Ravelston Dykes
Belford Rd.
Ravelston Pk.
Dean Cemetery
Water of Leith Walkway
Dean Path
B
Belgrave Crescent Gardens
2
West Mill Ln.
DEAN VILLAGE
Dean Bridge
2
Upper Damside
Miller Row
Bells Brae
2
Scottish National Gallery of Modern Art/ Modern Two
Sunbury Pl.
Belford Ms.
Damside
Well's Court
Belford Rd.
Lynedoch Pl. Ln.
Hawthornbank Ln.
P
Scottish National Gallery of Modern Art/ Modern One
2
M
6
Belford Pk.
Belford Rd.
Douglas Gdns.
Rothesay Ms.
Rothesay Pl.
Rothesay Terr.
Drumsheugh
Drumsheugh Gdns.
Mor
Surgery
Chester St.
Walker
2
Water of Leith Walkway
Belford Pl.
Water of Leith Walkway
Douglas Cres.
Eglinton Cres.
Glencairn Cres.
Grosvenor Cres.
Edinburgh Tutorial College
Palmerston Pl.
Melville St.
William St.
N.W. La.
St. Mary's Episcopal Cathedral
Manor Pl.
William S.W.
Wester Coates Pl.
Wester Coates Gdns.
St. Serfs School
(Ex-) Donaldson's School
Magdala Ms.
Magdala Cres.
Eglinton Cres.
Coates Gdns.
St. Mary's Music School
Grosvenor Cres.
Lansdowne Cres.
Rosebery Cres.
Rosebery Cres. Ln.
Grosvenor St.
Grosvenor Gdns.
Palmerston Pl. Ln.
West Maitland Street
Torph
Coates Av.
Wester Coates Rd.
3
West Coates
Stanhope St.
Stanhope Pl.
Devon Pl.
Haymarket Terrace
A8
Haymarket
P
DSS
A70
Morrison Street
P
Morrison Link
Otiso M
BURN
W. Catherine Pl.
Sutherland St.
Carberry Pl.
Borthwick Pl.
HAYMARKET
Haymarket Yards
Haymarket Station
Dalry Road
Dairy Pl. Cres.
4
d.
Sauchiebank
Russel Rd.
Easter Dalry Dr.
North St. Duff Pl.
Cathcart
Washington Ln.
Easter Dalry Rd.
West Park Pl.
St. Brides Cinema
Orwell Terr.
A70
Richmond Terr.
Caledonian Rd.
Caledonian Pl.
Caledonian Cres.
Orwell Primary School
Dalry Swimming Pool
Cinema & Megabowl
Dundee St.
5
McLeod St.
West Approach Road
Duff St. Ln.
Springwell Pl.
Downfield Pl.
Murieston Ct. Ln.
Murieston Cres.
Murieston Pl.
Murieston Terr.
Murieston Rd.
Dalry Road
Dalry Cemetery
West Approach Road
Dundee St.
Fountain Pl.
West
Yeaman Pl.
Gibson Terr.
Murdoch Terr.
Viewforth
Union Canal
Home Terr.
6
Gorgie Road
Tynecastle Ln.
Springwell Medical Centre
North Merchiston Cemetery
A70
St. Michaels
teford Road
Laurel Terr.
Ardmillan Terr.
Ardmillan Pl.
Angle Park
West Bryson Rd.
Dundee Terr.
Bryson Rd.
Ritchie Pl.
Henderson Terr.
Watson Cres.
Bryson Rd.
Temple Park Cres.
Harden Pl.
Methven Pl.
Polwarth Gdns.
Polwarth
MERCHISTON
McNeill St.
Thistle Pl.
Dorset Pl.
Gilmore
Granville Terr.
Merchiston Ms.
Merchiston
Montp
Castle Te
East
Merchiston Av.
0
200 m
300 yd
Harrison Park

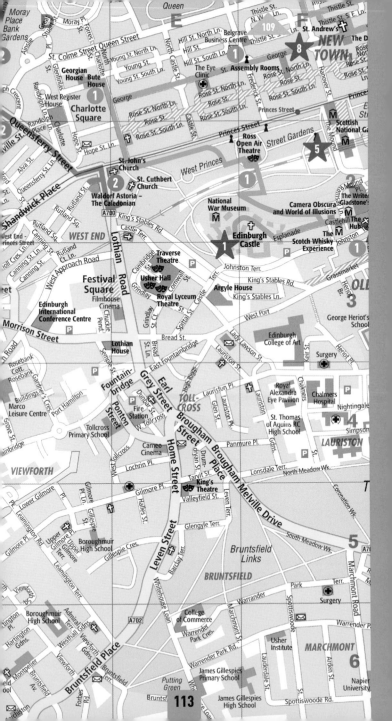

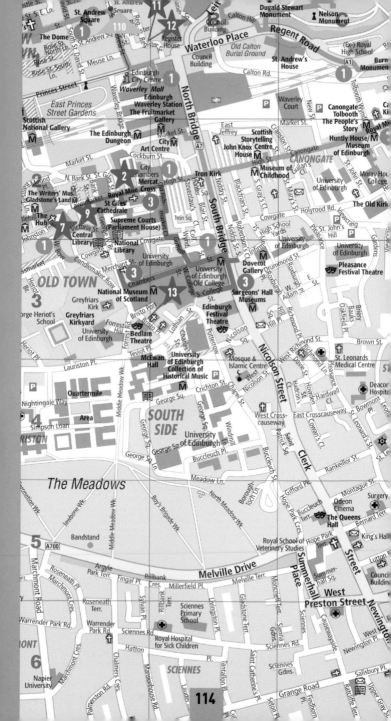

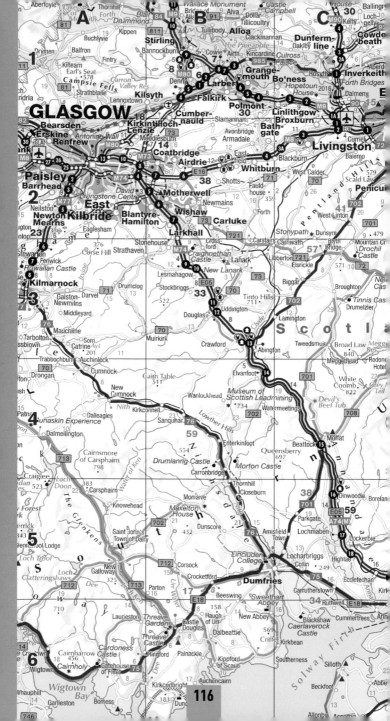

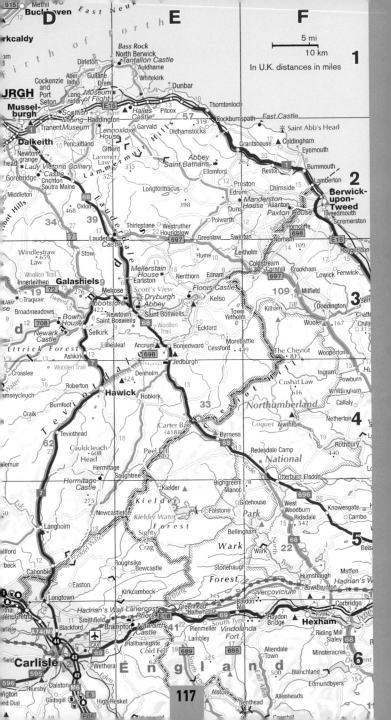

This index lists a selection of the streets and squares shown in the street atlas

Ⓜ	Museum
🎭	Stage / Bühne
ℹ	Information
✝	Church / Kirche
✡	Synagogue / Synagoge
☪	Mosque / Moschee
⊕	Hospital / Krankenhaus
✵	Police / Polizei
⊠	Post
📖	Library / Bibliothek
♟	Monument / Denkmal
🚋	Bus terminal / Busbahnhof
∴	Ruin / Ruine
🎾	Tennis court / Tennisplatz
🏌	Golf course / Golfplatz
🏊	Indoor swimming pool / Hallenbad
P	Parking / Parkplatz
⚠	Youth Hostel / Jugendherberge
▬▬	Railway with station / Eisenbahn mit Bahnhof
▨	Remarkable building / Bemerkenswertes Gebäude
▨	Public building / Öffentliches Gebäude
▨	Green / Grünfläche
□	Uncovered area / Unbebaute Fläche
▧▧▧	Pedestrian zone / Fußgängerzone
▬▬	Discovery Tour 1 / MARCO POLO Erlebnistour 1
▬▬	Discovery Tours / MARCO POLO Erlebnistouren
★	MARCO POLO Highlight

FOR YOUR NEXT TRIP...

MARCO POLO TRAVEL GUIDES

Travel with
Insider
Tips

INDEX

This index lists all sights and destinations, plus important streets and squares featured in this guide. Numbers in bold indicate a main entry.

WRITE TO US

e-mail: info@marcopologuides.co.uk

Did you have a great holiday? Is there something on your mind? Whatever it is, let us know! Whether you want to praise, alert us to errors or give us a personal tip – MARCO POLO would be pleased to hear from you. We do everything we can to provide the very latest information for your trip. Nevertheless, despite all of our authors' thorough research, errors can creep in. MARCO POLO does not accept any liability for this. Please contact us by e-mail or post.

MARCO POLO Travel Publishing Ltd
Pinewood, Chineham Business Park
Crockford Lane, Chineham
Basingstoke, Hampshire RG24 8AL
United Kingdom

PICTURE CREDITS
Cover photograph:Carlton Hill (Schapowalow/ SIME: R. Spila)
Images:Godiva (19 bottom); Rob Hoon (18 top); huber-images: G. Cozzi (4 top, 12/13, 26/27, 34, 48, 91), O. Fantuz (43), M. Rellini (82/83, 99); M. Kirchgessner (60, 65, 94, 96, 96/97); H. Krinitz (14/15, 30, 33, 97); Laif: Artz (24); Laif/Le Figaro Magazine: Goisque (74/75); Laif/Loop Images: J. Lorieau (103); mauritius images: Vidler (5, 23), mauritius images/age (110/111); mauritius images/Alamy (flap right, 2, 3, 6, 8, 17, 37, 39, 40, 56 right, 98 top), A. Buchanan (7); Mockford & Bonetti (18 bottom, 19 top, 76, 77, 79, 80); Schapowalow/SIME: R. Spila (1); T. Stankiewicz (flap left, 4 bottom, 9, 10, 11, 20/21, 44, 46/47, 50/51, 52, 55, 56 left, 57, 58/59, 63, 66/67, 68, 70/71, 73, 86, 94/95, 95, 98 bottom); Ian J. Watson (18 center)

3rd Edition – fully revised and updated 2019
Worldwide Distribution: Marco Polo Travel Publishing Ltd, Pinewood, Chineham Business Park, Crockford Lane, Basingstoke, Hampshire RG24 8AL, United Kingdom. Email: sales@marcopolouk.com
© MAIRDUMONT GmbH & Co. KG, Ostfildern
Chief editor: Marion Zorn
Author: Martin Müller; editor: Nadia Al Kureishi
Programme supervision: Lucas Forst-Gill, Susanne Heimburger, Tamara Hub, Johanna Jiranek, Nikolai Michaelis, Kristin Wittemann, Tim Wohlbold
Picture editor: Gabriele Forst
What's hot: wunder media, Munich; Martin Müller
Cartography street atlas and pull-out map: DuMont Reisekartografie, Fürstenfeldbruck; © MAIRDUMONT, Ostfildern
Front cover, page 1, pull-out map cover: Karl Anders – Studio für Brand Profiling, Hamburg; design inside: milch-hof : atelier, Berlin; Discovery Tours, p. 2/3: Susan Chaaban, Dipl.-Des. (FH)
Translated from German by Robert McInnes, Susan Jones, Tom Ashforth; editor of the English edition: Christopher Wynne, Lizzie Gilbert
Prepress: Nazire Ergün, Cologne

MIX
Paper from responsible sources
FSC® C124385

DOS & DON'TS ✊

How to not rub people up the wrong way in Edinburgh

DON'T WAIT FOR YOUR BEER IN A PUB

In a pub, you have to order your drinks and food at the bar and pay for them at the same time. The food is then brought to your table.

WAIT UNTIL THE LIGHT TURNS GREEN

Pedestrians have to press a button at a traffic light if they want it to turn green. However, the locals frequently cross when it is red if there is no traffic.

ONLY PAY FOR YOUR OWN DRINK

If you go on a pub crawl with a group of locals, there are always as many rounds as there are participants. The drinks are paid for in turn. So, make sure the group is small if you don't want to end up under the table.

DON'T CALL THE SCOTS ENGLISH

You are actually in Great Britain or the United Kingdom but definitely not in England. Don't forget to call the people *Scottish* even if *English* is on the tip of your tongue. By the way: Scotch is also incorrect: that's the drink.

DON'T ORDER SCOTCH ON THE ROCKS

There is always a jug of water on the bar in the Whisky Capital so that you can put a few drops in your drink if you want to. As a rule, the Scots think that ice ruins the subtle taste of the "water of life".

SHAKING HANDS

For non-Brits: if you look closely, you will notice that shaking hands is not very common in Scotland – especially with women. You introduce yourself with your full name and then often continue on a first-name basis.

DON'T DRIVE YOUR OWN CAR

Driving in the Old Town is often tricky business. If you don't feel like walking, catch a bus. That is what most of the locals do. You can buy tickets from the machines at the bus stops or, with the correct change, from bus drivers.

DON'T RAVE ABOUT GLASGOW

Don't let on that you think Glasgow is great. The two cities are completely different and there is no love lost between their inhabitants.

BUY THE RIGHT KILT

It's best to ask for a pattern that isn't associated with another family.

USE KNIVES IN PUBLIC

The Scottish knife law prevents the carrying and use of knives in a public place. Only pen knives with blades less than three inches in length are permitted.